THE STRESS WORK BOOK

How individuals, teams and organisations can balance pressure and performance

Eve Warren and Caroline Toll

NICHOLAS BREALEY
PUBLISHING

LONDON

First published by
Nicholas Brealey Publishing Limited in 1993,
156 Cloudesley Road
London N1 OEA

in association with
The Industrial Society
48 Bryanston Square
London W1H 7LN
Tel: 071-262 2401

© Eve Warren and Caroline Toll 1993
Illustrations by Paul Sands from ideas of the authors

ISBN 1 85788 0110

British Library Cataloguing in Publication Data
A catalogue record for this book is available
from the British Library.

Typeset by Bookworm Typesetting, Manchester, England
Printed and bound by The Lavenham Press Ltd,
Water Street, Lavenham, Suffolk

Contents

Other titles in the Series
COACHING FOR PERFORMANCE
A Practical Guide to Growing
Your Own Skills
John Whitmore

CONSTRUCTIVE CONFLICT MANAGEMENT
Managing to Make a Difference
John Crawley

POSITIVE MANAGEMENT
Assertiveness for Managers
Paddy O'Brien

Forthcoming Titles in the Series
COUNSELLING SKILLS AT WORK
Michael Megranahan and Rose Hull

EMPOWERING LEADERSHIP
Rob Brown and Margaret Brown

Acknowledgements

We would like to acknowledge the help and support of our colleagues in the Industrial Society as well as Cheryl Davies, Tony Manning, Liz Paton, Ray Toll, Bridget Wright and in particular Nick Brealey, who have all helped to make this a better book. Delegates on our stress management and women's development courses, and people we have worked with over the years have played an important role - by providing valuable insights into the management of stress at work. We would also like to thank Liz Bargh who initiated the book.

We are very grateful to our partners, Dennis Merrigan and Ray Toll, for their tolerance and encouragement while we worked on our own stresses in the process of writing!

WE DEDICATE THIS BOOK TO 'PEPPERELL'
WHERE WE FIRST WORKED TOGETHER
DEVELOPING STRESS MANAGEMENT COURSES

Introduction

There is much that we can do to manage stress. Whilst the subject means many different things to different people and can be hard to define, we provide both a straightforward approach to demystify stress and a guide to turn it to advantage. This book suggests how you can manage your own stress both in and out of work so as to achieve a healthy working life. It also identifies how, as a manager, you can help others to manage their stress effectively at work, achieving maximum benefit for both the organisation and the individual. It concludes with ideas that can be adopted within the whole organisation to make it stress fit.

The book is written from our experience of running workshops and training courses in many different organisations, and from working with individuals who want to take some control over their stress – including ourselves! It uses examples – either real or derived from real experience, with the names and contexts changed – and exercises that work in practice. The examples in Chapter 10 are all from organisations that responded to a small Industrial Society survey carried out in 1991 for the purposes of this book amongst organisations from a range of sectors and of different sizes.

Because we wanted the book to be easy to read there are not many references. We have credited ideas whose origins we know, but we are aware that we have absorbed and developed other people's wisdom in the course of our work.

We hope that you will be able to translate our ideas into practical action that will help you in the balancing act: managing your stress, maintaining good health *and* achieving effectiveness at work.

EVE WARREN and CAROLINE TOLL

PART I

STRESS AT WORK

Stress Fitness 1

'Stress costs industry millions each year.' A newspaper headline proclaims the bottom-line implications of this modern malaise.

LOST WORK TIME

In *The Mind Survey: Stress at Work* (Mind, 1992) a fifth of companies attributed up to 50 per cent of all days off sick to stress-related illness. It has been estimated that 100 million working days are lost each year in the UK in the same way (Fletcher, 1988). To put stress into perspective, this is significantly more than the days lost in 1991 through industrial action (Bird, 1992). A recent CBI/Department of Health conference report (1992) identifies that thirty times as many working days are lost as a result of stress-related mental illness as are lost from industrial disputes.

   Many claims have been made of the recent surge in stress-related work absence. One estimate puts the increase since the mid 1950s at 500 per cent (Boyes, 1987). Both the costs to industry and the effects of stress are difficult to measure accurately. One suggestion is that up to £20 billion is lost each year as a result of stress (Coleman, 1992).

PERSONAL COSTS

As well as affecting the economy, stress has personal costs. Disease, mental health problems, drug abuse, alcoholism, fractured relationships, career stagnation, boredom, dissatisfaction and unhappiness can result.

USING STRESS CONSTRUCTIVELY

Management of stress at work is essential if employers wish to make the most of people's potential. However, this means more than just dealing with the disruptive effects of stress – absenteeism, high turnover, low commitment, indecision and poor communications.

We can tackle the issue constructively if we appreciate that stress has its positive side, its healthy dimension, as well as its more frequently accepted downside. Stress management means harnessing the energy of healthy stress as well as minimising the unhealthy outcomes. Because the type and degree of stress that people experience at work will affect their performance and consequently the achievements of the organisation, stress management is integral to good management practice.

YET ANOTHER STRESS BOOK?

Nearly half the companies responding to the Industrial Society survey for this book cited low morale and absenteeism as negative indicators of stress in the workplace. If stress is one of the major influences on performance at work, then why is more not done to manage it?

Part of the problem is that stress is assumed to be negative. We shy away from the topic, believing that to be suffering stress reveals a personal weakness. Colleagues may react with embarrassment, imply that we should 'pull ourselves together' or be apparently concerned but do nothing to help. In such circumstances it is no wonder that stress gets hidden ... and in so doing we continue to associate it with the idea of weakness.

Stress may be talked of generally in the workplace; indeed some cameraderie may be created by the shared experience of being under pressure. However, it is difficult to recognise it in ourselves unless we learn to attune to the signs. More commonly we struggle on, not recognising the pressures building up, not accepting our limitations. We can appear to be coping – until our stress levels reach crisis point. The consequences – an outburst, mistakes or days off sick – create even more stress for ourselves and for others.

The alternative is to admit to pressure and to needing help. The anticipated reactions of immediate colleagues and one's manager will affect our willingness to open up. Will we be met with sympathy and practical support? Or will it mean a black mark against us? Stress may damage your health and work but admitting to it, it seems, might damage your career.

The manager has the power to bring stress into the open and help others to deal with it constructively. This of course can be difficult if the manager is also under extreme stress and is in part responsible for creating pressures. These may have built up from both inside and outside the workplace: the MIND survey found 93 per cent viewed stress as a symptom or manifestation of personal or work problems. The job still needs to be done, but the manager may well feel powerless to help, and may not understand that a member of staff's private life can affect their ability to work.

Similarly, relationships with colleagues, management styles and systems and the organisational culture will affect the incidence of stress, either creating, exacerbating or diminishing pressures at work. Stress is a reality in the workplace – and we can generate it by the ways we organise things and deal with people.

Because each person's experience of stress is unique, each one will react individually, and so it is difficult to quantify the effects. This makes it a problem to produce guidelines for managing stress. Couple this lack of awareness with feelings of unease and we can see why dealing with the topic is often avoided. However, it is possible to build up a dossier of both individual and organisational indicators to provide insight into the stress levels: a stress health check. Organisations that choose to work on stress management strategies usually have some indications that they are needed.

WHAT YOU CAN DO TO BEGIN MANAGING STRESS

- Understand that stress management is integral to good management practice

- Recognise that stress has both positive and negative aspects: both need to be managed for enhanced performance and benefits at work

WHAT IS STRESS?

When asked to define what 'stress' is we may well come up with words that describe how we might feel, such as tension, anxiety or panic, or the things that cause us to feel in this way – the pressures and their implications in our busy lives, both in and out of work. Stress has come to mean both the causes and the effects of feelings of pressure. However, this general view of stress can cause confusion and mislead. There may well be positive or negative results arising from a stressful situation. In this book we shall be using 'stress' as a neutral term to describe the experience of reacting to pressures.

To understand what stress is, it is useful to consider the constant experience of demands made on us and our ability to meet those demands.

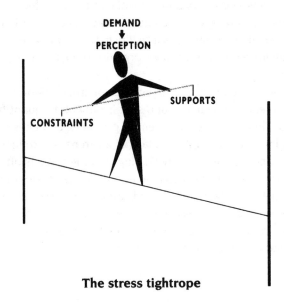

The stress tightrope

- a *demand* is made on us;

- *constraints* that limit our capacity to meet the demand make it seem greater;

- available *supports* help us to meet or manage the demand;

- the demands and the constraints create *pressure*;

- the effect on us is *stress*.

It is the interpretation of demands, constraints and supports – perhaps unawares – that determines our stress response.

Each one of us will see the situation through our own eyes and it is our perception of the demands, and our ability to meet them, that will determine whether we are feeling 'stressed' or not. Our responses will be influenced by what else is going on at the time. Thus the interplay of constraints, demands and supports is endlessly variable. The same situation may or may not lead to stress for an individual at any given moment in time. **Stress, then, is a response to the perceived relationship between the demands on us and our ability to cope.**

Example: Chris

Chris has been given a complex new project by his boss. His reaction, his approach to dealing with it and ultimately his performance will be coloured by a number of different factors, including perhaps:

- what Chris thinks about his job and the part it plays in his life
- whether he feels sufficiently skilled to cope with the work involved in the new project
- whether he sees the project as an opportunity for career development or as a tedious extra chore
- whether he is interested in the project or not
- how he feels about his boss and what he thinks of her motives for giving him the project
- what control he perceives he will have over how the project is to be managed
- whether he is healthy and fit or feels he is going down with the flu
- what else is going on for him in his life outside work – perhaps a family wedding, financial troubles, a house move, a sick child, an ageing parent
- how his organisation is faring at the time, whether buoyant and optimistic or recovering from the last round of redundancies.

Whilst there is no objective measure of how anyone will or should respond to a situation, we can learn to attune to our responses, and the demands, constraints and supports in our lives, and use this awareness to create more control over the circumstances and our reaction to them. When we feel stressed we often feel out of control; identifying what is going on is an important first step.

WHAT YOU CAN DO TO UNDERSTAND YOUR STRESS

- Consider that stress arises from the interplay of demands, constraints and supports

- Recognise that managing stress involves a balancing of these elements

- Recognise and intervene in the build-up of pressures

- One way of doing this is to think of the last time you felt really pressured and list:

    - the demands

    - the constraints

    - the supports

- Can you prevent this situation building up again? What were the warning signs? Can you think of any action you could take to correct the imbalance?

- If not, read on ...

THE STRESS CURVE

The traditional stress curve identifies understress, healthy stress and overstress and their relationship with our performance. Because each person is individual, each curve is likely to be a different shape.

If we feel too little stress, for us at that time, our effectiveness will reflect our understimulation and will be reduced. We are all aware of those moments when we feel bored or lethargic, have no enthusiasm for the day or the job, and feel unmotivated or frustrated, represented by (1)–(2) on the curve. Perhaps we do not have enough demands, or the work is too easy. The expressions, commonly heard, that 'I work better under pressure' or 'I give my best work when the heat's on' encapsulate this **understress**. Interestingly, in such circumstances we sometimes generate greater pressure for

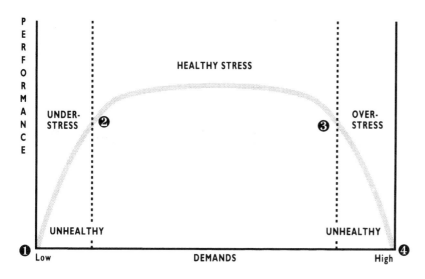

The stress curve

ourselves by leaving a tight deadline for a project and then
having to pull out all the stops to complete it – giving an
enhanced performance in the process.

As our stress increases, our energy generally rises and our
performance grows until we reach our optimum stimulation –
for us at that moment. In this area on the curve, (2)–(3), we are
performing at our absolute peak. We feel stimulated, excited
and challenged by the opportunities presented by a demand,
appropriately in control, and with the right amount of variety
and change for us. This is when we deliver our best work. We
are in **healthy stress** and feel at our most satisfied.

However, if this goes on for too long – or the pressure
increases either in or outside work with inadequate supports –
we hit a point where we will begin to be overstretched and
overstimulated, at (3), and where our performance will
diminish. Then we begin to feel that the demands are too great,
that we cannot fulfil our commitments – and our feeling
becomes reality as we experience **overstress**. We may begin to
behave in ways that in themselves sabotage our performance.
Perhaps we procrastinate, pick arguments, work exceptionally
long hours with little to show for it, delegate ineffectively, have
difficulties in sleeping, or sleep too much, and fail to view
things with our normal clarity.

Long-term overstress can lead to physical and mental illness
with their potential consequences of absence from work and

personal suffering, as well as lessened effectiveness in the process. If we fail to heed the warning signs then we can get into areas of personal breakdown and exhaustion near (4). Our reactions and the links with physical illness will be covered more fully in Chapter 2.

STRESS FITNESS

In the same way that we are able to cope with physical and mental activities more or less effectively, so our ability to cope with stress will depend on our level of stress fitness.

If we are physically active at work, we need to have a certain level of physical fitness to equip us for the job. In addition, actually doing the job will build up our fitness. Ensuring that we are healthy and that our bodies are fit and well enables us to meet the demands of the job and generally maintains and extends our fitness level.

In a job that relies less on physical effort but more on mental or intellectual activity, the daily and routine demands of the job will be less tangible but will also require a level of ability or fitness. This can be developed in the same way as we develop our physical fitness: through training, practice, application and learning.

In both types of job, additional pressures will arise in the form of extra demands: a difficult customer to handle, an increased workload because of an unfilled post, a new challenge in which to prove one's potential. By developing our ability to withstand temporary extra pressure – by increasing our stress fitness – we will help ourselves through the tough patches. Stress fitness protects us from the harmful effects of overstress and will also guide us out of understress. Just as an athlete works consistently in training, so we have to work on our stress fitness.

To stay physically fit we need to be using our bodies appropriately and caring for them. If we push ourselves too hard or neglect our physical health we are very likely to suffer from strain. The same applies to us as whole people. If we are not stress fit, we will have greater difficulty in coping with excess demands.

WHOSE RESPONSIBILITY?

Whilst individuals have responsibility for their stress, so organisations too must play their part.

Example: Nicky

Nicky, a new and promising employee, is not working as effectively as expected and there is an uncomfortable atmosphere in the office. No one says anything until there is a row between Nicky and her secretary over a minor point. Work is interrupted for quite a while with both unhappy about the situation. In discussion it turns out that there is uncertainty between Nicky and the secretary about responsibilities and duties, with each thinking that the other is making life difficult and duplicating effort.

Unnecessary stress has been created by unclear briefing and lack of clarification – the responsibility of the manager. Similarly, by raising the issue earlier both parties could have prevented the build-up of unhealthy stress.

Example: Simon

Simon, previously very meticulous about his work, suddenly began to make mistakes. This led to others having to doublecheck his figures and eventually the manager warned that he must improve. It emerged in discussion that Simon had financial problems and was expecting his home to be repossessed. The worry was adversely affecting his performance. There was little that his manager could do to help – except listen to his concerns and temporarily ease the work pressures, instead of piling them on further.

Understanding how the pressures are generated and accumulate, seeing each person as an individual, alerting oneself to the signs of over- or understress and taking steps to keep people in the healthy stress area will enhance performance and make for good management practice. Such an approach recognises that stress is a fact of life – and a positive tool for motivation and work quality.

If we wish to harness this source of energy we have also to admit to and acknowledge its negative effects – not as weakness but as examples of poor management. Perhaps we can help our colleagues or staff as well as ourselves to keep healthily stressed.

WHAT YOU CAN DO TO HELP OTHERS MANAGE THEIR STRESS
● Accept that stress is the responsibility of both organisation and individual
● Ask yourself how you would react if a member of your team or a colleague said they were feeling overstressed
● Consider what support you could offer

The Effects of Stress 2

Stress effects

There are generally several ways in which stress responses manifest themselves:

- our *bodies* may react automatically or we may be able to manage them by our thoughts;

- our *thoughts* will be sharp or confused;

- our *feelings* will become motivating or destructive; and

- our *actions* will demonstrate either our best abilities or counter-productive behaviour.

FOR EXAMPLE

The following examples are typical of reactions to stressful situations, although not everyone will respond in exactly the same way.

If we are threatened with losing our job:

  – our heart begins to thump
  – we see our employer as acting unfairly
  – we feel frightened of the consequences at home
  – we begin to behave less cooperatively.

In other words, we are beginning to be overstressed, heading for unhealthy stress.

If we initiate new projects:

  – we will be poised for action
  – we will be thinking clearly
  – we will be excited
  – our work will be of a high standard.

This means we are healthily stressed.

When we do not have enough to do:

  – we are lethargic
  – we are depressed
  – we feel we are of no value to anyone
  – we are reluctant to do anything.

This would be a case of understress, but there is also the possibility in this situation that:

  – we may be full of unused energy
  – our thoughts may be racing
  – we feel frustrated
  – we behave aggressively.

Either way we are in a state of unhealthy stress.

BODIES

When we lived in caves or in the wild it was very important to deal with the physical threats all around. If a wounded hairy mammoth or sabre-toothed tiger turned on us we needed to pursue the attack effectively, run flat out in the opposite direction or hide behind a rock and remain motionless but ready for instant action if necessary. This automatic reaction may still be life-saving; if there is a fire in the building we can jump a flight of stairs that we would not be able to manage at another time. Adrenalin plays a large part in this.

FIGHT, FLIGHT, FREEZE – OR MANAGE

Example: Peter

Peter had been invited to reapply for his job as there had been a take-over. On the way to the interview, he found that his heart was thumping. While he was waiting to be called his hands were sweating so much that he had to wipe them surreptitiously before he shook hands with the interviewers, and, while talking, he found himself short of breath.

The difficulty we face these days is that the effort we are required to make is not usually entirely physical, but our bodies still respond in the same way to pressures and prepare us for action. The difference is that now we can become aware of what is happening. This makes it possible for us to find ways of changing our perceptions (see Chapter 5) and responses so that we can manage them effectively. If that is not possible we can at least take care of ourselves in ways that help us to avoid the ill-effects of too much pressure or too long an exposure to it.

AT FIRST

In simple terms, when the brain registers that a demand is being made and that an effort is needed it triggers reactions in the body that include a release of various hormones. There will be different combinations of hormones depending on the type of event and how we see it. The physical responses usually affect the following:

Heart   beats faster to pump the blood more quickly to the relevant parts of the body and to supply more energy

Blood   the pressure rises as a result of the heart's increased activity
clotting agents are released into it to decrease bleeding from wounds

Lungs   the rate of breathing is increased to keep up oxygen
        levels
Liver   cholesterol is released to provide energy
Brain   more blood flows to it for quick thinking
Senses   become more alert to warn of danger
        pain reactions are dulled to protect initially if there is
        physical harm
Skin   blood leaves it to minimise bleeding from wounds
        sweat helps to keep the body cool
Muscles   receive more blood to supply energy for action
Digestive system   is not needed during action, so less blood
        reaches it
        bladder and bowels empty as they are not needed
Sex organs   are not needed so less blood flows to them
Immune system   is often affected

The important thing to remember is that these responses, in
themselves, do no harm if we are using them actively or if there
is a relaxed period after the effort has been made so that the
body can return to its normal state.

NEXT

If our stress continues or increases and more energy is needed,
then other hormones are released into the blood stream. The
combination of hormones will depend on whether we see the
demand as welcome or unwelcome. These help to make more
energy available from the stores in the body, in the form of fats
and sugars. Again, if these are used actively then no harm is done.

However, if no physical activity takes place, or there is no
resolution of the pressure, then the fats may attach themselves
to the walls of arteries, leading to chronic high blood pressure.
One of the ways of preventing this is to take exercise so that
the fats can be used up.

LATER

If there is no respite then the more harmful effects of stress are
likely to be felt. The stores of energy will become exhausted if
not given time to re-stock. This is when our bodies have been
in overdrive and are more likely to seize up. At this point the
only remedy initially is complete rest and then a gradual
building back to health.

Example: Jeannette
Jeannette is a middle manager in a construction company
where the attitude is that people should be able to cope.

If employees 'fall down on the job' or are taking a lot of time off then they are seen as incompetent and not worth keeping on. The firm's products are connected with the defence industry so, when the defence forces were cut back and the market began to shrink, many of the staff realised that their jobs would be on the line.

Jeannette found that she was having moments of breathlessness, which alarmed her, but she felt that it was such a minor complaint that she did not mention it even to her husband. Then she began to have palpitations too, particularly on her way to work. She simply did not understand since she had always been very fit and these 'weaknesses' were out of character. She struggled on for several months then had to make several of her staff redundant. Eventually she collapsed in her office and had to be rushed to hospital.

Jeannette had not noticed that her symptoms were those of overstress and that she was being badly affected by the combination of threats to her own and her staff's jobs, as well as her unhappiness at having to make some of them redundant.

It seems that we each have our own level of available energy. While one person may be able to keep going for a long time, someone else will have to stop much earlier.

Many illnesses have been shown to be stress-related and a great deal of research has been done, particularly on the connections with heart disease. But we often seem to go down with other illnesses as a result of stressful times. Even though the stress may not have been the cause, resistance has been lowered so that we are more vulnerable.

CONSEQUENCES

Early on, however, there are other signs that all is not well. Physical symptoms may include these reactions:

- palpitations
- breathlessness
- headaches
- skin trouble
- sweating too much
- indigestion
- many colds
- raised blood pressure shown up at a medical check
- feeling too hot

- over-sensitivity to noise or smell
- muscle cramps
- loss of sexual desire
- disturbed sleep

Many of these are connected with the areas of the body affected by the automatic response. There are many other signs of being under pressure. It is important to learn to recognise our own particular ones as they are helpful in alerting us to what is happening. This then gives us time to think about managing ourselves and deciding what we can do.

One of the main things is to have a medical check-up. While the signs may be showing us that we are beginning to suffer from the overstress, they may also have other causes which might need medical attention.

If we are unaware of our responses in being unhealthily stressed, or if we ignore them, then we are unlikely to recognise the need to do something to restore balance.

WHAT YOU CAN DO TO MANAGE BODY RESPONSES

- When you are under pressure or experience a stressful event, notice where in your body you feel the effects

- Begin to identify what situations make you feel like this

- If you cannot use up the physical energy at the time, make sure you release it constructively later through exercise

- Have a check-up with your doctor at the first signs of discomfort

- See Chapter 7 for more ideas.

THOUGHTS

When we are able to rise to a challenge our thinking is clear and creative: we are able to work out how to solve problems, what the priorities are and strategies for working effectively.

If the pressure continues too long, we may suffer from mental overload. Our thoughts become confused, we cannot see the wood for the trees and we may be so anxious that we cannot make decisions.

This is a sure sign that we need to take stock. We may need only to get into the habit of walking round the block, breaking for a few minutes, doing something different or taking a quiet lunch reading or chatting to restore a sense of perspective and stop the unproductive way thoughts are going round and round in our heads. When our minds are hyperactive or confused we are likely to act in ways that are not effective. We are then probably passing on the stress to others. When this happens we need to step back from the situation, take stock of what is happening and decide what to do about it.

There is some evidence that, by using our thought processes, we can help to mitigate some of the body responses to pressure. Some people who meditate or use other techniques find they do not automatically respond physically in ways that are harmful to them.

WHAT YOU CAN DO TO HELP CLARIFY THOUGHTS

- Actively distract yourself with a break, a crossword, a book or some other activity

- Talk to someone about what is worrying you

- Get some more ideas that will help from Chapters 5 and 7.

FEELINGS

Some people consider that feelings have no place at work. There is also often a tendency to pretend, to ourselves and others, that there are no feelings around. But this denies the value of enthusiasm, enjoyment and excitement, and we all know what it is like to work alongside people who are clearly angry or upset but who are not doing anything to sort out the difficulty.

Example: Christine

Christine prefers to keep her feelings to herself. She believes that, at work, she should respond with courtesy at all times and tries very hard to stay equable and good humoured. She sometimes feels pulled in lots of different directions during the course of her working day, and does her best to meet the demands of others. As a line manager she needs to work with people above, below and level with her in the hierarchy but at busy times she can feel by the end of the day that she has no more resources to call on.

She has been known to snap at her staff, but on the whole she keeps herself to herself. Increasingly she is feeling exhausted in the evening and hasn't much energy for her husband or children. She sometimes feels that the demands on her are too much to handle. However, she thinks that she just needs a good holiday and then things will be better. Nevertheless, it seems like a long time before that can happen and she thinks perhaps she needs a tonic to pep her up.

Example: David

David believes in letting off steam. He is proud of this aspect of his character and sees part of his managerial role as injecting energy and dynamism into the proceedings. He shows his feelings by laughing, shouting and sulking; whatever seems natural at the time. It is not uncommon that he will bawl out a team member in public or show his delight in something by hugging the nearest person. He is sometimes exasperated by the reserve of his colleagues and can't understand why they don't let on how they are feeling. In particular, when he asks someone how they are feeling he gets confused when they just say 'OK'.

At home his family behave in a similar fashion. Emotions are expressed immediately, grudges are never held, resentment is unheard of and everyone is comfortable with his volatile temperament, unlike at work.

In many organisations, unwritten rules have developed about the place of feelings at work and, for many people, the expression of feelings, positive and negative, can cause discomfort. At the same time, to stay healthy and stress fit, feelings need to be acknowledged and dealt with constructively.

That is not to say that anger or frustration, or even joy and delight, should always be expressed when they happen; there are appropriate times and places for this. But, if the cause is not addressed, then the build-up inside can lead to an outburst at an unsuitable moment, which can be destructive both to the individual and to the organisation. When the feelings are channelled positively then they can become strong motivators for creative problem-solving and building good relationships.

WHAT IS ACCEPTABLE

There are some stereotypical ideas about expressing feelings and what is acceptable for each gender. Often the tearful response of women stems back to childhood when it was clear that girls were allowed to cry but not show anger; as a result, even if they are angry, some women burst into tears. Equally, many families accept that boys may be angry but must not cry. This conditioning can be inhibiting for both genders. The danger is that people can become cut off from acknowledging their own feelings. The result is that they are likely to be insensitive to others. The 'stiff upper lip' can also lead to high blood pressure, mental disorders and unsocial behaviour. It usually means that real issues are being avoided and serious situations arise that could have been prevented because we have not noticed the build-up of internal pressure.

Too often if we show our feelings we are seen as vulnerable, weak or out of control. We need to recognise that we are all a mixture of physical reactions, feelings and thoughts, each of these affecting the other. For example, when we are depressed we think everything is terrible, we feel extremely sad all the time and our energy levels are down. We all feel low from time to time, but when depression stops us from leading our normal lives then we are in need of professional help.

The same applies to anxiety, which can become all pervading. It is normal to be anxious at certain moments and it is part and parcel of managing healthy stress, somewhere at the interface between challenge and threat. But when we are anxious about everything, then there is usually an underlying cause that can be worked through with the help of trained therapists.

WHAT YOU CAN DO TO HELP WITH FEELINGS

- Learn to notice when feelings are building up

- Recognise that they are part of being human and a useful signal to you

- Find times and places when it is appropriate to express them. Ideas in Chapter 7.

- If you find your feelings spilling over in inappropriate places, or if you are bottling up feelings until they explode, consider choosing one of the ways of releasing the tension and developing ways of dealing with the feelings:

    - chat things over with a good friend who listens to you seriously and accepts your feelings

    - talk to a counsellor

    - work out a strategy for dealing with situations that cause you difficulty, with someone you can trust

    - let out the feelings in a safe place

ACTIONS

When we are healthily stressed we work efficiently and make good progress. The quality of our work is of a consistently high standard. We are cooperative and get on well with colleagues.

The way we and others behave, physically and verbally, is often the first sign that we are beginning to suffer from the harmful effects of over- or understress. We may become withdrawn, be irritable with everyone, or make silly mistakes.

This can help us to recognise that we need to do something to stop the ineffective behaviour before we lose our jobs or begin to affect other people's work. Sorting out what is causing us to act in an unhealthy way is the beginning of finding a way to remedy the situation. Time taken to do this, perhaps with someone else's help, can be very productive and prevent us reaching a point that makes it more difficult to pull ourselves up again to normal activity.

WHAT YOU CAN DO ABOUT ACTIONS

- Try to identify any specific behaviour that creates more pressure or allows unwelcome stress to continue

- Work out, perhaps with someone else's help, what triggers your behaviour

- Find strategies for managing your body, thoughts and feelings, as outlined in this chapter

- Recognise how important it is to say 'no' to unhealthy stress and to develop assertive behaviour to help with this

- Read Chapters 5, 7 and 9

In the same way that our initial responses to a pressure may begin in one of the four areas outlined, we can begin to manage our stress in any one of those areas. But we need to make sure that we monitor our bodies, thoughts, feelings and actions to regain or maintain health in its widest sense. This concept is discussed more fully in Chapter 7.

3 It's Only a Job ...

STRESS AT WORK

The term 'pressure' is generally used when people talk about such positive aspects of their work as achieving results against the odds, pulling out all the stops to meet a project deadline or coming up with successful solutions in really difficult circumstances. On the other hand, the word 'stress' usually refers to unpleasant aspects – the difficult colleague, the seemingly insurmountable mountain of work, the unattainable deadlines or the unrealistic expectations of the boss: in fact, anything that creates feelings of discomfort, unease, overload or being stretched in too many directions. Yet, as we have seen in Chapter 1, stress can have both pleasant and unpleasant effects. If we expect and want the healthy buzz of pleasure, then we have to accept that sometimes it can overwhelm and harm us – as outlined in Chapter 2. Learning to manage our stress involves both minimising the negative and the damage to our health and also maximising the positive as well as our fitness and performance!

All jobs contain a potential for stress. The dealing room, the classroom, the casualty department or the factory floor might be thought of as typically high-pressure environments, but even the quiet office, the home or the showroom can provide high stress levels. Whilst we can identify common pressures in any workplace, the determinant of the stress level is the person who experiences it. Given the constantly changing relationship between demands, constraints and supports, and how they are seen by the individual, it is easy to see how stress levels will also change over time.

When we are feeling under pressure it can be difficult to identify the reasons. Indeed, the whole picture can seem like a bit of a jigsaw, with all the pieces interlocking, which of course is exactly how our lives are. Pressures will arise from a unique combination of elements. Any of these can (a) please us and meet our needs and preferences, (b) broadly satisfy us, or (c) cause concern and dissatisfaction. They can act as demands themselves (for example the tasks expected in our workload or the need to travel to the next appointment); they can serve as constraints that stop us meeting the demands (as when our dissatisfaction with our career progression or concern for our job security preoccupies and distracts); or they can support us

RECOGNISE THE PRESSURES

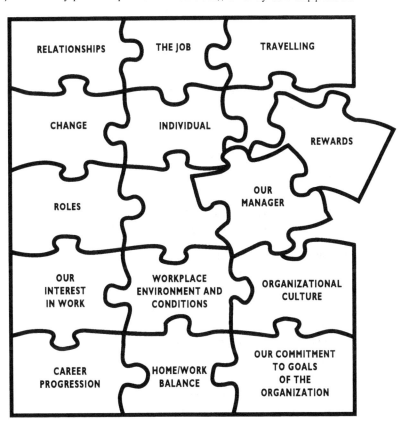

The pressure jigsaw

(for example, our commitment to the work or excitement in the new job boosting our energy and capacity). The degree of *control* we have over the pressures in our lives and the amount of *information* we have about what is going on are two themes that run through all of the above.

CONSTRAINT OR SUPPORT?

High demands, many constraints and few supports are the classic ingredients of unhealthy stress. Whilst being ill-informed and out of control will seem like additional constraints, being in the know and gaining some degree of control – if only of our reactions – will support us and help tip the balance.

Feeling powerless to control events is a common experience of unhealthy stress. Exercising some degree of choice in the demands and constraints – having a say in the pressures – serves to reduce their impact.

Example: Sean
Sean is a supervisor in a small firm.

Control/choice
- he is unable to influence decisions that affect his work
- he gets conflicting demands from several managers
- he has too much work, which affects his ability to do it adequately
- he is directed to do it in a way that is against his better judgement
- he has difficulty in getting the resources to do the job properly
- he does not have enough authority or the skills required for the job assigned to him, and no training is available
- his career and progress depend on his boss's decisions

Communication/uncertainty
- he is unsure of the business climate and the issues affecting it
- he is unclear how the department fits into the organisation
- he is unsure about his job role and its boundary
- he is unclear about goals and targets for his team and himself
- he rarely receives praise or helpful criticism
- he rarely talks freely with his boss or colleagues so conflicts are not dealt with, resentments build up, mistakes are hidden and difficulties are ignored

It is worth making a special point about change. Welcome changes can give us real stimulation and healthy stress, yet when someone else is initiating the change, and it is one we do not welcome, extreme pressure can be felt. This is particularly so when we personally can see no reason for the change, as is often the case with organisational changes. Tensions as a result of a restructure or reappraisal of our role are a common pressure and, here again, the information we receive will have an impact on our perception. Whether we perceive threats or opportunities in the change will affect us.

The rate of change in the business and how it is managed will be significant in an organisation's stress levels. There will be times when a whole organisation is under threat, either from internal factors such as restructuring, or from external forces such as a recession or a new competitor in the market. At such times, the pressures of uncertainty, lack of influence and control plus fear of what the changes might mean to individual jobs can generate a wave of stress, which, if not effectively handled, can have great impact on the ability of the business to keep working and survive.

Some of us are better equipped to cope with our own changes and to introduce change to others. However, we can learn to handle the process so that those affected are supported through it. There is more about managing change in Chapter 8.

THE IMPACT OF STRESS AT WORK

ON THE ORGANISATION

A significant factor in any organisation's success in changing times is the skill with which its people deal with stress. Stress can seriously affect the organisation's achievement of its goals. It is a critical feature too in employee involvement and team effectiveness: the healthily stressed colleague is more effective; unhealthily stressed employees are a cost burden reducing their own as well as, potentially, colleagues' performance. Thus the style with which the manager tackles the issue of stress – so that it does not become a problem – is vital, and of course how the manager's own stress is managed will also have an influence.

It is often considered that unhealthy stress plays a part in absences from work and a recent study identified a higher absence rate in Britain than in any other European country. Interestingly, more than 40 per cent of UK businesses do not measure absenteeism at all (Arthur Andersen, 1991). Similarly only 14 per cent of respondents in the Industrial Society survey had any sort of policy statement about stress management.

Work is often thought to be just those activities for which we are paid. Yet the person running a home and family full time, studying or doing voluntary work will certainly see what they do as work and in this book we include such activities in the term 'work'.

For many of us, work plays an important part in our lives and our relationship with stress. Work generally dictates the time-frame that structures our days, and provides them with some sort of focus. It will, for many of us, determine where we live and when to move. Directly or indirectly it will represent for most of us the means whereby we purchase what we need or want. It also may bring other rewards, including a sense of value or importance and a social definition, in the eyes of ourselves or of others. By putting us in touch with other people, in certain places, engaged in specific activities, it focuses or influences the structure of our lives. As such, if work is not going well, the unhealthy stress can be profound.

It is very easy for work pressures to spill over into the other parts of our lives and for the flow to go the other way, from home to work. Our lives do not neatly compartmentalise as we might wish them to do. What is potentially serious is when work dominates us, taking up a far greater proportion of our thoughts, energies and efforts than is commensurate with its relative importance in our lives. The regular encroachment of work into our own time – our family and leisure time – during the week, at weekends and in holidays suggests an imbalance, with too much emphasis on work for health. Allowing an imbalance to establish itself in our lives can have serious long-term implications. We need to ask ourselves whether we are *living to work* or *working to live*. This is expanded in Chapter 6.

Example: Dianne

Dianne had been with her Education Authority for fifteen years and had successfully progressed her career within it, reaching a Senior Inspector's post. She had always taken her responsibilities seriously, with the effect of neglecting other areas of her life; she felt that she had little time for hobbies or social activities apart from those connected with work. Weekends were often taken up with chores or family visits and she frequently brought work home. Extra pressures were tackled by working even longer hours.

When the Authority reorganised and she was encouraged to take early retirement she was devastated. She had given total commitment to her work and had very little to put in its place. Unhealthy stress she had experienced in her job continued into her retirement.

Our ability to manage ourselves, our work and our relationships in the organisation will affect the achievement of our work goals. By redressing any imbalance in the interplay of constraints and supports, we will be more able to meet the demands, thus building up our stress fitness. Sometimes, however, we cannot do this for ourselves and need help in the process. Our colleagues or manager can often provide some additional support. However, if our relationships at work serve as further demands or constraints, then we shall be descending further into overstress. How we react to colleagues will be significant in whether stress gets passed around the workplace, infecting others, or gets effectively managed in its early stages.

Unless we identify behaviour as indicating stress, then our reaction to it can well exacerbate the situation and generate even more pressure, for ourselves and for others. Thus stress infects an environment where people work together. This means that unhealthy stress is spread in all directions: sideways, downwards, upwards and outwards.

THE STRESS VIRUS

Example: Craig

Whenever things went wrong on the production line in a busy factory, the project manager, Craig, would fly off the handle, blame anyone who came near him, and spend much longer over lunch in the pub than usual, coming back definitely the worse for wear. Long-standing members of his staff generally kept their heads down until the storm blew over but meanwhile time was lost in production. Newer members of staff were sometimes upset by Craig's accusations.

Clients were dissatisfied with late deliveries and this came to the notice of the sales director, who inevitably put more pressure on Craig to keep up with the schedule. This stress virus was only halted when Craig's boss heard what had been happening and helped him to work out a system for solving problems when they arose with the help of key people on the factory floor.

Workplaces where stress has not been managed constructively will tend to be places where there is little trust, not much cooperation, bickering, blaming, and probably a high rate of absenteeism, sick leave and turnover of staff; in other words, very unhappy and unproductive places for work.

WHAT YOU CAN DO TO HALT THE STRESS VIRUS
● Be aware of stress in the workplace
● Check your own reactions to someone else's stress. Make sure that you are not passing on the virus
● Watch, listen and intervene at an appropriate stage to halt the virus

THE STRESS VACUUM

Just as overstress can be a problem at work, so daily exposure to a working environment of persistent understress – the stress vacuum – can have the effect of sucking us in and dragging us down. It is hard to maintain a sense of optimism and purpose in working climates in which boredom and apathy seem to be the norm.

Such workplaces are characterised by the 'safe' approach to tasks and problems, with a complete avoidance of any calculated risk-taking. People will not be pushed or developed – although they may well stay a long time – and their performance will not benefit from the healthy drive provided by well-managed stress. We need to guard against the stress vacuum as well as the stress virus.

WORKING STRESS LEVELS

The Henley Centre found in their 1990 survey that stress was a major concern in the workplace. For high earners, the stress the job caused was identified as the least pleasant aspect of the job (cited by nearly 40 per cent), followed by travelling to and from work and long hours – in themselves pressures. For those in lower income brackets the most overwhelming concern was with the level of earnings, followed by travelling and then the stress caused by the job.

Each of us has need for stress, but what is too much pressure for one can be exciting, stimulating and challenging for another; what is a comfortable level of pressure for another can be mindlessly dull for someone else. Our stress needs will reflect our own personal profile and similarly, as individuals, we may well find these needs met from our work – or from other aspects of our lives.

For most of us, decisions regarding our working lives are made with no thought at all to stress. However, given the connections between performance and stress, in order to do our best work consistently the job must allow opportunities for appropriate stress.

Whilst our jobs may be characterised by lots of demands, this healthy stress might still prove elusive because the demands are insufficiently challenging, the constraints predictable or minimal, or the supports too many. In such circumstances unhealthy stress is generated by being at odds with the job.

Not only is persistent overstress unproductive, it is potentially personally dangerous. Often the unhealthy stress generated from work pervades and harms all areas of our lives so that we are not functioning as we would like or gaining the enjoyment and satisfaction we want from our own time. Allowing the stress to continue unabated means we are denying ourselves the opportunity to change in ways that benefit everyone: family, friends, ourselves, our colleagues, our employers. Ignoring stress can mean we allow work completely to influence and infect the rest of our lives.

Just as we need to consider many aspects when taking a job, it is helpful to recognise that stress problems arise when person, job and organisation do not fit. Working in an environment that is at odds with our preferences and stress needs will lead to dissatisfaction – from either under- or over-stimulation.

Healthy stress is more likely to result when there is a good person–job fit. When the type of demands and the overall balance of constraints and supports suit individuals and their stress needs at that moment, extra energy enables even greater achievements and a healthy whole life.

Our need for stress, unfortunately, is rarely taken into account in career choice. Nor is the changing nature of jobs generally recognised and planned for. As job demands change we can often adapt to cope with mismatches for short periods. However, if there is a significant mismatch of person and job or

ARE YOU GETTING ENOUGH?

HAVE YOU GOT TOO MUCH?

FINDING THE RIGHT LEVEL

person and organisation, in the long term we will be heading for reduced performance and potential understress or overstress, unless we take action to change the situation.

WHAT YOU CAN DO TO CHART YOUR WORKING STRESS LEVELS

Use the following chart to identify your stress levels within your present working role. Scores at or towards either end of the scale will reveal whether you are overall in understress or overstress, i.e. your person–job fit is not entirely satisfactory now. Consider whether you can take action to improve this, and who could help. Alternatively, do you need to explore options to change your present working situation?

position too secure, path predictable and mapped out	1 2 3 4 5 6 7 8 9	position and organisation insecure
too few demands	1 2 3 4 5 6 7 8 9	too much to do
tasks too easy	1 2 3 4 5 6 7 8 9	tasks too hard
too quiet	1 2 3 4 5 6 7 8 9	too noisy
repetition & little variety	1 2 3 4 5 6 7 8 9	too much variety
boredom	1 2 3 4 5 6 7 8 9	many different projects on the go
too little travelling	1 2 3 4 5 6 7 8 9	too much travelling
too little progression	1 2 3 4 5 6 7 8 9	fast career track
too little influence, control or responsibility	1 2 3 4 5 6 7 8 9	too much influence, control or responsibility
too little interest or involvement in work	1 2 3 4 5 6 7 8 9	too much interest or involvement in work
over-managed	1 2 3 4 5 6 7 8 9	under-managed

couldn't care about work	1 2 3 4 5 6 7 8 9	totally committed to work

SCALE:

UNDERSTRESS 12..............60..............108 OVERSTRESS

For healthy stress you will need to be somewhere in the middle, i.e. scoring around 60. However, notice any extreme scores and consider whether these are balanced out by the other scores and the situation is generally satisfactory.

WHERE IS THE STRESS?

It is often thought that greater pressures are experienced the further up the organisational hierarchy one goes. It is true that, as we move up the organisation, pressures of a particular nature increase, for example associated with decision-making, accountability and ultimate responsibility; so too, however, do opportunities for control and influence, which can prove to be great supports. Many people feel that stress is handed down in a hierarchical organisation. Since we are employed to work, this involves being put under some pressure, yet it does not have to be harmful.

Different types of pressure are experienced throughout the organisation. At management levels, for example, there will be pressures to perform from one's own manager, and pressures generated by one's team and their work problems and concerns. At the lowest level in a hierarchical structure there will be pressures from above to produce work of a certain quality and quantity, with generally fewer opportunities to influence or change the context. Research by Professor Cary Cooper and Dr Rosalind Bramwell (1992) shows a high incidence of stress-related absence among shopfloor workers. In one brewery there were two and a half times more absences than among managers. One of the issues cited was a feeling of being undervalued.

In some organisations there may be pressures arising from communications and work schedules. For the self-employed or small business person the pressures will be integral to work generation and delivery. Public sector pressures often stem from government-imposed changes and new legislation, as well as public comment and criticism. It is no surprise that teachers and health service personnel have experienced overstress after numerous new initiatives and public discussion of their working practices. Such workers also, by the very responsive nature of their professions, are dealing at all times with the demands of different groups of people, with little power to make any impact on resourcing or additional supports. Similarly in the voluntary sector, limited resources and even greater demands produce overstress. The pressures, though specific to the nature of the workplace, will have elements in common.

As organisations become leaner, jobs tend to expand and create further demands. In these circumstances it is all too easy for stress to be handed down the line in the form of bad planning and weak management, and back up the line in the form of blame and sabotage in both overt and more subtle forms. The first signs of such things getting out of hand will be shown in the individual responses listed in Chapter 4.

There are many specific occupational pressures associated with work and our careers and these will be explored more fully in Chapter 6. However, by considering the demands we experience in our jobs, and the constraints and supports that operate both in and outside the workplace, we can begin to analyse our stress levels and those of the individuals in the teams we manage.

PLOT THE PRESSURES

The checklist of the pressure already identified at work can help us to identify our own stress. For all the categories on the checklist unhealthy stress can be generated for individuals as a result of their own experience, perception and particular workplace context. Whilst people's tolerance of these factors will vary, they can have an impact at any level in the organisation.

CHECKLIST: PRESSURE POINTS

- **Workplace environment and conditions**
  light
  privacy and space
  air freshness and quality
  resources and equipment
  standard of accommodation

- **Travelling**
  journey to and from work
  essential regular travelling within the job
  adequate resources for this, i.e. vehicle, recognition
  of time taken
  budgets

---

cont.

- **Intrinsic to the job**
  nature of work
  overload or underload
  specific demands in job
  extent of decision-making

- **Roles**
  clear or vague boundaries
  shared or conflicting expectations
  clarity of job descriptions
  extent of responsibility clear or not

- **Our manager**
  how we are managed
  approachable or not
  his/her own stress levels

- **Rewards**
  pay
  appraisal
  acknowledgement

- **Relationships** with:
  colleagues
  manager
  subordinates
  people within the organisation
  people who influence our careers
  those we need to do our job

- **Our interest in work**
  levels of involvement
  satisfaction with job
  variety and pace of work

- **Our commitment to the goals of the organisation**
  belief in the 'business'
  any conflict with the values or methods

- **Organisational culture**
  expected behaviour
  extent of communication and consultation
  internal politics and power relationships
  management style

cont.

- **Career progression**
  career development
  promotion
  fear of redundancy, retirement, relocation
  organisation's view of career path and its links with reality
  thwarted ambition
  extent of influence
  job in/security

- **Individual**
  personality type
  in/ability to cope with change
  un/equipped with essential skills for work
  coping strategies for difficult situations
  suited or not to work and organisation
  suited or not to position in the hierarchy
  willingness to learn and change
  stress fitness

- **Home/work balance**
  conflicting demands
  one interfering with the other
  time constraints

- **Change**
  at work: confusion about new technology
           expansion, diversification
           relocation, slimming down
  at home: accumulation of life events

WHAT YOU CAN DO TO IDENTIFY YOUR PRESSURES

- Refer to the pressure points checklist and consider your own work situation

- Identify the categories where unhealthy stress is created

- Overall how satisfied are you with your stress levels?

- Where you have identified dissatisfaction, what action could you take to reduce the pressures?

- What action could you take to build up your supports?

- Read on for further ideas!

PART II

STRESS AND THE INDIVIDUAL

Pressure and Performance 4

Although the focus of this book is mainly stress at work, what is happening outside work will have an impact. In particular, changes in our lives have been shown to affect our well-being in the long run if attention is not paid to looking after ourselves when they happen. The research, conducted originally by Holmes and Rahe (1967), identified a list of stressful events that seemed to affect the health of those who experienced them.

The following are the 'top 10' life events:

1 Death of a partner
2 Divorce
3 Marital separation from partner
4 Detention in prison or other institution
5 Death of a close family member
6 Major personal injury or illness
7 Marriage
8 Being fired from work
9 Marital reconciliation
10 Retirement

Some of the other events that come further down the scale are shown in the table on p.43. Not all the events would be considered unpleasant or undesirable; indeed many are positively welcome. However, they all involve change, for either better or worse; for example, promotion and demotion can affect what we are able to do, and with whom, both at home and at work. Life changes also involve elements of loss or gain, and our reactions will depend on which of these seems to be most powerful at the time. Moving home may involve losing contact with friends and family, a familiar environment and a particular lifestyle; on the other hand it could mean gaining in these areas. For one individual the move will be traumatic; for another, exciting.

The extent of the change involved, the balance between loss and gain, and the extent of the control we have over what is happening will be influential in determining how we respond to the major and minor events in our lives. Similarly, our reaction will be affected by our general state of physical health and state of mind when the event occurs.

Example: Jennifer

Jennifer was able to cope with a high level of pressure in her job and had shown that she could rise to challenges effectively. Her role as manager of operations in a manufacturing plant meant that she balanced all sorts of demands, led a strong team and coped with being the only female manager on her level with few apparent problems. She had been identified by her manager as a 'fast tracker', and had always willingly and competently accepted extra projects, which signalled her competence and ambition. Thus her manager was surprised when one of these extra projects came in way over deadline and with glaring errors. Jennifer herself seemed reluctant to talk about her poor performance and then went off sick with a heavy cold – something she had never done before, always struggling into work even when sick. This was admired in the company.

Her manager began to wonder if she really had the capacity to cope in such a job, and whether she'd been promoted too soon.

Jennifer was trying to keep her own problem situation, out of the picture at work. She did not want to explain that her father had just died, and that she was having to

Examples of stressful life events

Personal events	Either	Work events
Pregnancy		Business readjustment (merger, reorganisation, bankruptcy)
	Change in financial state (better or worse)	
Death of close friend		Change to different work
	Taking on a mortgage	
Son or daughter leaving home	(for a home or business)	Change in responsibility (promotion, demotion)
In-law troubles		Troubles with boss
	Outstanding personal achievement	
Spouse beginning or leaving work outside the home		Change in working hours or conditions
Moving house		
Change in amount or type of recreation		
Change in sleeping or eating habits		
Holidays		
Christmas (and other religious celebrations)		

make all the practical arrangements and take care of her mother as well. She feared that her boss would see her reaction as a sign of weakness, and misinterpret her grief as just feminine emotion.

Anxiety about her job created more pressure – and she was not sure to whom she could talk. If, she felt, her boss would just accept the situation, then she could ask for some help. But she was concerned how it would be seen by her company.

We need to recognize not only the impact of single events but also the cumulative effect of life changes and the disproportionate escalation of pressure when a number of these changes occur together, in sequence or in close proximity. This happens because we have not had time to readjust to the first event before another happens that draws on our energy reserves. Each of us has only so much energy available at any one time. We can respond to challenges and are often surprised at how long we can keep going in a crisis, but at some point that energy must be replaced. At such times we need to pay even more attention to our stress fitness and ensure we allow ourselves the time to stand back from stressful situations.

Similarly, routine day-to-day events can constrain us as we struggle to meet our other demands. A disrupted journey to or from work, collapsed childcare arrangements, property repairs to be organised or domestic chores to be fitted into a busy schedule can all affect our performance at work.

WHAT YOU CAN DO TO FACE UP TO CHANGES

- Be sensitive to the number of life events, in both your own and others' lives

- At times of potential overstress because of significant or numerous changes, build up your rest periods and supports

- To do this you need to talk about the situation. If you can, challenge a work culture that pretends such pressures are unimportant, by acknowledging their impact in both your own life and the lives of your colleagues

- Work towards creating a work climate in which it is possible to outline the significance of particular changes if they affect performance. This involves acknowledging that people have lives outside work that will affect their work performances

- If you cannot understand why a colleague is not performing to peak, find out if life changes are the key

- Appreciate the variety of responses to change in our lives. Some of us will be excited by changes, some will find them unsettling. Accept the differences in responses, and allow yourself the time and space you need to accommodate the change into your life. Allow this for others too

SAY 'YES' TO STRESS

To ensure an appropriate balance between our demands, constraints and supports over a period of time we need to be aware of their accumulation and our reactions, aiming to keep in healthy stress and away from the under- and overstress areas. This is illustrated by the following variations on the traditional stress curve shown in Chapter 1.

When we are understressed, one of two things will be happening. Either we are not getting enough stimulation to keep us healthy and the result is lethargy, boredom and a body that is not functioning efficiently, or we may be frustrated, losing self-confidence and feeling angry with a body reacting to the internal stress generated as though in overstress. In fact we may be taking a short-cut from near the beginning of the stress curve to the other end of the curve. In neither condition will we be stress fit.

Stress fitness requires that we increase our capacity through training. Just as when learning a new sport we will take it one step at a time, so to move out of the understress area, we should view progress as a series of Steps. With gradually greater demands, performance will improve, although a period of readjustment or levelling out will usually be necessary to accustom ourselves to the new load and develop our skill, before further demands will be effectively met. Support, training and increased pressures will help performance to rise,

UNDERSTRESS AREA:
THE STEPS

though results will not necessarily be seen immediately. Our stress health will improve as we climb the Steps.

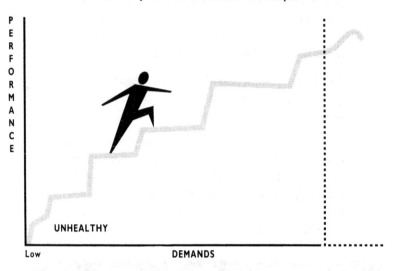

The Steps

Example: Sam
On the Steps
Sam had been taken on as a trainee manager by a chain of large stores. After some time his supervisor noticed that he was becoming unhelpful, working only the minimum number of hours and sometimes arriving late. He wandered round with nothing particular to do and when asked to take on simple tasks he was reluctant, finding excuses to avoid them.

When Sam was tackled by his supervisor he became truculent and claimed he was being picked on. He also volunteered that he did not seem to have energy for anything and suggested he might be unwell. Subsequently however he kept postponing appointments with the doctor.

The supervisor had a brainwave and asked Sam to work with one of the managers of a large department to redesign the layout so that customers could see the goods more clearly as they came in. Sam's demeanour changed rapidly and the departmental manager was delighted with his innovative ideas. So Sam was able to move from the bottom of the first area and climb up his first Step.

Once we reach our optimum stress levels, where we are experiencing our most effective and satisfying performance, we are in the Peaks. This healthy stress response keeps us stimulated, excited, feeling challenged and appropriately stretched. Yet keeping going at the same heights will lead to overstimulation and burnout.

By learning to lower our output from time to time, and by deploying a range of strategies for the body to manage the effects of the stress response, and coping strategies to rejuvenate, we can be prepared afresh for the next demand – and maintain our peak performance.

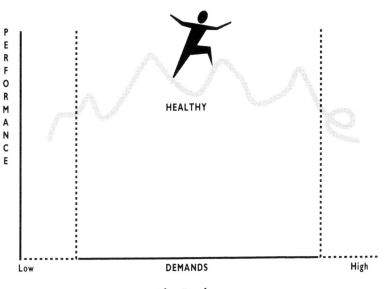

The Peaks

Example: Philippa

In the Peaks

Philippa had joined a construction company straight from college. She had shown such promise that she had been encouraged to get further qualifications, supported by her employers. As her career progressed, she achieved considerable success within the company.

She was working on a large contract with colleagues. The team helped each other out when there were deadlines and were always sparking off ideas with each other, adding to the quality of their work. There always seemed to be a positive atmosphere in their team and they clearly enjoyed working together. Philippa had worked her way up the Steps and was managing her way through the Peaks very successfully.

OVERSTRESS AREA: THE SPIRAL

We can often cope with short bursts of intense pressure, particularly when we can see an end in sight. There are specific projects with limited lives, reports to write, standard returns that recur regularly and many other events that we can generally cope with most of the time. The trouble tends to occur when the demands continue for a long time with no end visible and we have no control over them.

If we do not look after our stress fitness whilst moving through the Peaks, we are likely to overstretch ourselves and reach the overstress area. It is very difficult from this point to stop oneself sliding down the overstress Spiral.

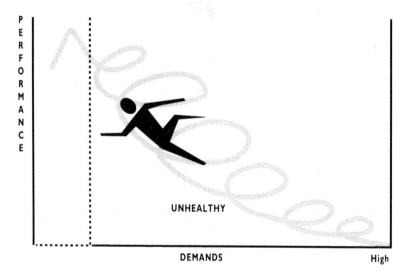

The Spiral

Example: Terry

Down the Spiral

Terry was a very conscientious and reliable worker in the maintenance section of a large garage, working a lot of overtime. Although he had good friends he had been doing nothing outside work. He used to enjoy music but had not played, listened to his tapes or been out for ages. His thoughts were always on problems and difficulties at the garage. He was not sleeping well and was getting indigestion but kept thinking that these would get better, not noticing that this had been happening for months.

One day at work he collapsed and was rushed to hospital where the doctor told him that he had narrowly escaped a heart attack. While he was recovering he was encouraged to eat a more healthy diet and pick up his music again with his friends. He was also able to negotiate more manageable hours at the garage since they did not want to lose him. Terry had been helped to pull himself back from very near the bottom of the Spiral to nearer the Peaks again.

The type of stress experienced by the individual and the length of time over which it is experienced are the two factors that add to the likelihood of the sequence continuing. Once in unhealthy stress, our reactions to the experience will usually in themselves generate more pressure – either for ourselves directly, or for our associates – sending us (and others) even more rapidly down the Spiral. Our performance will diminish, and we may well eventually be unable to work at all because of physical or mental illness. It is a slippery route down – and we need to admit to overstress and take practical steps to prevent the downward Spiral. Understanding what happens helps us to be better prepared for stress when it occurs and better equipped to stay in the Peaks.

WHAT YOU CAN DO TO MOVE THROUGH THE STRESS CURVE

What you can do on the bottom Step

- Tackle the causes of being there

- Look for more challenge either in or out of work

- Talk to your boss and/or someone who could help

- Build up new skills to climb the steps

- Use the strategies in Chapter 7

What you can do in the Peaks

- Watch out for warning signs and act on them

- Look after yourself in ways that use up surplus energy and keep you stress fit (see Chapter 7)

---

cont.

- Make sure, if you hit a particularly high peak, that you have time to recover

- If you feel that you are approaching the Spiral take immediate action to avoid it

What you can do in the Spiral

- Immediately slow down the pace

- Talk to your boss and/or someone who can help

- Identify and tackle the causes of your reaching this point

- Resolve and plan to use regularly the strategies in Chapter 7

- Start straight away!

WHAT TO LOOK OUT FOR

One of the most significant signs of a move into unhealthy stress is a *change* in someone's health or how they are thinking, feeling or behaving. It is generally easier to identify these in ourselves, even before they become clear to other people. But we need to be sensitive to changes in other people if we are to appreciate what is happening to them and to be able to help. One of the difficulties is that, when we are experiencing any of the symptoms of unhealthy stress ourselves, it can be almost impossible to be alert to signs in other people. We are often so caught up in our own troubles that we have no energy or attention to spare.

Example: Amanda

Amanda has heard that there are to be big changes in the clothes manufacturer where she is a designer. To prove her worth she works very hard and produces greater numbers of innovative ideas. At the same time she becomes increasingly impatient with her colleagues when they do not pick up on her ideas quickly and she upsets clerical staff by expecting them to respond to her demands immediately. Amanda's reactions to the threat of changes are being expressed in her thoughts, feelings and actions. The importance here is that she has changed since the mention of upheavals in the firm.

In the ordinary bustle of work it is very easy to be unaware of, miss or ignore the warning signs – at the expense of our long-term performance. We are so concerned to meet the deadline, get through the pile on our desks, make sure we are keeping up with the work programme or meet the targets that we feel it is an indulgence to take any time out. This means that we press on regardless, in spite of the indications that we need to watch the balance in our lives. Awareness of the signs of unhealthy stress is the first necessity and the following checklists will help to develop an understanding of what we need to be looking out for if we want to maximise performance.

SIGNS OF UNDERSTRESS

These are some of the signs that may be experienced at the beginning of the Steps stage on the stress curve. They do not follow a set pattern and will clearly not all be shown by one person, but they can serve as warnings.

CHECKLIST: SIGNS OF UNDERSTRESS

- low self-esteem
- irritability

- unreliability
- lack of decision-making
- irregular attendance
- confused thinking

- low energy

- lack of enthusiasm

- tiredness
- critical attitude expressed.
- disgruntled manner
- simple errors
- little interest in work
- moaning about situation but no action to change it
- taking extra time to produce work
- taking excess of stimulants

As progress is made up the Steps, signs of healthy stress begin to appear.

SIGNS OF HEALTHY STRESS

When we are under the amount of pressure that suits us in the Peaks, our state of well-being is one that most people would like to achieve. It is also the one that produces the best work.

CHECKLIST: SIGNS OF HEALTHY STRESS	
● good concentration	● appropriate sense of humour
● cooperative behaviour	
● high standard of work	● enhanced achievements
● effective problem-solving	● strong interest in business and job
● deadlines met	● good long-term planning
● good information flow	● clear thinking
● clear and confident decision-making	● high level of motivation
	● realistic about self
● harmonious relationships	● plenty of energy
● good attendance and time-keeping	● positive comments
	● constructive criticism given and received
● cheerful manner	
● concern and care for others	● feelings of being valued and competent

There will be low levels of mistakes, accidents, outbursts of anger or tears, backbiting, gossip, worry, fear or anxiety, except when justified. There will be no alcohol or other drug abuse, minimal sleep problems or unnecessary absences.

SIGNS OF OVERSTRESS

Once we begin to slide down the Spiral there are many ways we can recognise what is happening. These are particularly significant if they are *changes* from our normal way of being.

Because our reactions are individual, some of these signs will be shown by some people and not by others, but they can all be pointers to a state of being that may become harmful.

CHECKLIST: SIGNS OF OVERSTRESS

- lack of concentration
- memory losses
- poor decision-making
- worry, anxiety or fear shown
- depression
- inconsistency
- not meeting targets or deadlines
- irregular attendance and time-keeping
- low self-esteem
- ineffective problem-solving
- lower standards accepted
- over self-critical
- losing business
- customer complaints
- poor long-term planning
- lost orders
- no sense of humour
- confusion
- bad mistakes
- regularly working late
- constantly taking work home
- easily disgruntled
- uncooperative relationships
- poor work quality
- emotional outbursts
- unreasonable complaints
- frequent criticism, gossip or backbiting
- unpredictability
- tiredness
- cancelling annual leave
- frantic bursts of energy
- extreme mood swings
- only concern shown is for self
- accidents
- eating difficulties
- greater use of alcohol, caffeine, nicotine, drugs
- difficulties with sleep
- low interest in work
- no one wants to work with person
- physical illness

In each of these stages our thoughts, feelings and actions may be affected; it is rarely the case that we experience only one response on its own. The interaction between body, thoughts, feelings and actions is endlessly variable. However, recognising the impact of stress will help us to achieve our best performance over time.

WHAT YOU CAN DO TO RECOGNISE THE SIGNS

- Become aware of your own stress responses

- Consider how they change as you move through the areas

- Notice others' behaviour

- If you think others may be on the Steps or heading for the Spiral, find out more about their situation, how they feel about it and if you can help

- If they seem to be in the Peaks, find out what brought them there and what they are doing to maintain their effectiveness

- Read on to find out more about stress at work and how you can manage it

---

The Inside Story 5

According to a Chinese proverb, two-thirds of what we see is
behind our eyes. Our perception and interpretation of a
situation will affect our response to it. The demand may seem
so huge that the effect will be great, or so small that it can be
easily managed. A focus on the constraints will highlight the
difficulties; a focus on the supports will mean the constraints
are hardly noticed. These ways of seeing will affect each
individual's experience of stress.

How people arrive at their own perception of events
depends on many factors, including their personality and what
happened in similar past circumstances, so it is not surprising
that we each react differently. Self-esteem – how we feel about
ourselves and our ability to cope – will also play its part.
However, it is important to recognise that where individuals do
not seem to be reacting in an expected way there will be an
internal rationale to their particular responses.

Example: Henry and Tony
A member of the team is leaving and, for economic
reasons, is not being replaced. Her work will have to be
divided between the other team members. Henry, who is
at present coping well, feels that this presents an

opportunity to build up his skills and add to his cv; Tony, however, feels so overloaded at the moment that he cannot cope with any more work. In reality their workload is similar. Different influences in each one's life have affected their perceptions.

Just as we can learn to recognise our physical reactions, so we can learn to understand and manage our inner responses – and intervene to generate the most appropriate response. By attending to and taking more control of what is going on in our thoughts and beliefs, in our behaviour patterns and in our feelings and attitudes, we can build stress fitness and dispense with or reduce harmful responses.

Taking some control of the situation and our reactions acts as a support, helps us feel better about the stress and is in itself a coping strategy. To be able to do this we must believe that it is possible to take some control. The extent to which we can achieve this will depend on whether we see ourselves as able to influence events in our lives, or as powerless to create change. Much of stress management relies on making adjustments to cope with the pressures in our lives and thus stems from the belief that it is possible to change.

In contrast, we also need to recognise what we cannot change, and this clarity of view is an important part of the managing response. Whilst we cannot always change or influence external events, we can change our interpretation and what we do about them. How to achieve this, and what to do when the situation cannot be changed, will be dealt with later in this chapter.

INTERNAL PRESSURES

Underpinning most of our actions are beliefs about what we can and should do that will have been acquired during our lives. The belief that we should be rational and reasonable at all times may exacerbate our tendency to unhealthy stress. Another belief is the expectation that we should always be right and never make a mistake; a third is that we should be liked by everyone. We often apply these pressures – demands and constraints from inside us – to ourselves and to others.

We may have been taught that we must never upset other people. However, in the course of work it may be necessary to give someone information that is likely to upset them. Instead

of constructively working out the best way to tell the person
what they would prefer not to hear, and to deal with the
consequences effectively, we often put it off, dash in clumsily
to get it over with or get someone else to do it. None of these
strategies is helpful to the other person we are concerned
about and we are causing more unhealthy stress to both than is
necessary.

Having ideals can be a very positive motivating force as long
as we do not insist on meeting them all the time. Perfectionists
often pressurise themselves unnecessarily and cause those
around them pressure too. How often have we thought, or
heard someone say:

'I must do everything perfectly.'

'Everyone else should have the same high standards as me.'

'My staff/children must do better than everyone else's.'

'I must make sure everyone likes and admires me.'

'Managers who have problems are incompetent.'

Such expectations can only lead to disappointment.
Tolerance of others and acceptance of ourselves are essential
if we are not to live in a perpetual state of dissatisfaction and
unhealthy stress. It is possible that we do not think we have a
right to be fallible. Clearly in some occupations, such as
medicine, fire fighting and social work, mistakes can be fatal. In
such jobs, which are likely to be extremely stressful, it is vital to
build up a range of supports so that the really important
demands are met.

In jobs that have less of a life and death dimension, the
perfectionist view can create all sorts of counter-productive
tensions. Those anxious to make absolutely no mistakes will be
reluctant to learn anything new or take the risk of a new
approach, losing opportunities for innovative solutions. Those
who will never admit to feeling under pressure will find it
difficult to ask for help when needed, with possibly disastrous
consequences.

Standards, though necessary and desirable, are unlikely to
be conformed to by all, and we will not always reach them.
Recognising when we have done well enough and allowing
ourselves to be less than perfect are powerful ways of reducing
the internal pressures, both at work and in our personal lives.

WHAT YOU CAN DO TO CHALLENGE INTERNAL PRESSURES

- Become aware of your internal pressures

- List as many of them as you can. Every time you find yourself thinking or saying 'I must do that' or 'you should do this' consider if it is a pressure you impose on yourself or others and if so put it on the list

- For each item on your list see if you can replace the belief with another – not too different – which reduces the pressure, e.g. expecting everything done to 100 per cent perfection could shift to settling for 85 per cent perfection

- When you find yourself building up the pressures on yourself with your beliefs, pause and reassess the situation and question the belief. Then replace it with your new one

---

CONFRONT YOUR OWN CRITIC

Accepting and caring for ourselves not only helps our stress fitness but also, in the long term, has the effect of boosting self-esteem. Expecting high standards all the time, and that we should never be weak, makes it hard to confront our needs. 'I should be able to cope' is a common view. Accepting that we cannot cope might seem a blow to our sense of self-worth, but as long as we go on pushing ourselves and denying our needs we will be heading for potential damage to our health, both physical and emotional. This erodes self-esteem.

We often allow our inner voice – the thoughts that go on all the time – to criticise and put us down rather than to support and value us. For example:

'I never do anything well.'

'Think of all the things that could go wrong.'

'Nobody thinks I'm any good.'

'I'm bound to make a mistake.'

Such thoughts act either as further demands or as constraints. Learning to like and love ourselves – to use our inner voice to support and affirm us – is tied in very closely with stress, both the cause and the response. Replacing these negative thoughts with more positive yet realistic ones will help our stress fitness.

If we are not feeling good about ourselves and our self-esteem is low we will not be able to act on many of these ideas. This is particularly true if we depend on other people's opinions for our feelings of self-respect. When this is the case we spend a great deal of time and effort trying to please other people and not necessarily doing what is needed in our jobs.

CREATING A PERSONAL STRESS CODE

One way to challenge the internal pressures is to consider and develop for ourselves a personal framework of guiding principles or beliefs that determine what we believe is acceptable for us. These beliefs will underpin relationships: our expectations of others and ourselves in relation to others. They will specify the value we place on people and the value we give to ourselves. It is important, however, that we translate these beliefs into behaviour: our own and that which we expect from others.

Finding the balance between what we believe and what others believe can be difficult, especially where our work role is involved. Assertiveness, a useful skill, is based on the extent to which individuals assert their rights and acknowledge the rights of others. If we are compromising and meeting each other half way we shall be more likely to arrive at positive solutions than if we pursue our own goals regardless or give in to everyone else's wishes all the time.

A sense of beliefs – a personal code – is an important part of stress management. It helps us to clarify what we believe holds true in relationships, it can identify personal limits and boundaries, and it does away with doubt about how we should be or act. The beliefs or guidelines in the box overleaf can provide a basis for action in those situations where pressure can be created. Each belief carries with it the responsibility of applying it to others.

VALUES AND VALUING

WHAT YOU CAN DO TO CREATE A PERSONAL STRESS CODE

Consider the following beliefs. Either reflect on them individually or discuss in a group or with another person the ones you subscribe to.

● I am worth being treated with respect

● I deserve to be listened to and taken seriously

● I can express views that are different from other people's and accept the consequences

● I am able to express feelings and accept the consequences

● I can say 'no' when I feel it is justified without feeling guilty

● It is all right for me to ask for what I want, although I accept that I might not get it

● I can make mistakes, try to correct them and learn from them

● I can admit ignorance and, if appropriate, will be prepared to learn

● I can act as I believe is right as long as it does not harm anyone else

● I can choose not to act on any of these beliefs (choose – not find excuses for not acting on them!)

Example: Janis

Janis often found herself overloaded at work and spending her free time doing favours for other people. When she discussed this with colleagues on a stress management course she realised that she was trying to please others and had not thought about what was good for her. She was not valuing herself and her needs, and she rated other people's opinion of her higher than her own. By working on what was important to her – her personal stress code – she was able to define her limits and boundaries, build her stress fitness and boost her self-esteem.

The following beliefs relate very specifically to preventing the build-up of pressure, for both ourselves and others. The responsibilities apply particularly to the manager's role. Implicit in them is the element of choice. We do not have to act on these beliefs; indeed in some circumstances the anticipated consequences might decide us against them. However, they may point out areas where our stress fitness is at risk if we do not tackle the beliefs we hold or that are held in the workplace or the home.

- I can leave at a reasonable hour using any benefits of flexi-time and have a responsibility to ensure my staff do so

- I can take my breaks and holiday and have a responsibility to ensure my staff do so

- I can ask the reason and give reasons

- I can delegate work

- I do not have to absorb others's unhealthy stress

- I can take time to reflect and take stock and allow others to do this

- I can ask for help and give it when needed

- I should reward and be rewarded

- I can challenge others' perceptions of me and be prepared to listen to others' views

- I can be wrong

- I can express my dissatisfaction or disagreement

- I can admit my vulnerable points to my boss or family

- I have a responsibility to manage my time and resources

- I have a responsibility to monitor my own well-being and build my stress fitness

- I have a responsibility to monitor the well-being of any staff I manage

WHAT YOU CAN DO TO WORK ON YOUR BELIEFS

● Use the lists above as starting points to develop your own personally relevant stress code, paying particular attention to those areas you have difficulties with

● Recognise that belief is one thing, action is another

● Recognise that acting on the beliefs will depend on the circumstances

● Use the beliefs to guide your inner voice in difficult times. For example, if there is a lot of pressure to work late and you are not prepared to miss an important social or leisure occasion, repeating to yourself: 'I have a right to say no', can prepare you to renegotiate the current expectation about working late

PEOPLE PRESSURE

We may find that it is particular people who cause us pressure, either by making what seem to be excessive demands on us or by relating to us in a way that we find difficult. This of course can cause even greater pressure when we have to work with the person.

Close proximity and frequent contact with someone we find difficult can lead to unhealthy stress as we strive to deal with our reactions to the behaviour we do not like. This is sometimes called a 'personality clash', a term that implies that we can do nothing about it. In our attempts to improve the situation, we may well wish that the other person would change, and, consciously or not, try to get them to do just this. Because our attempts will generally be unsuccessful, this can create even more frustration and unhealthy stress.

In such awkward relationships it is vital to recognise that we cannot expect to change anyone else. All we can change is our own reaction to the situation or person. Recognising what behaviour is causing the difficulty, and identifying that it might be their problem and not ours, means we have just our own response to manage – and nothing more.

Of course we also need to consider that some of our behaviour might have a similar effect on the other person and might be provoking their behaviour. To improve the relationship it can be helpful to open up the communication channels and discuss the behaviour that is affecting each one, using the 'Giving and Receiving Feedback' framework discussed in Chapter 8. This is particularly important if we have to work with the person.

If we try everything in our power to improve the working relationship to no avail, then we may need to explore 'Letting Go' (later in this chapter) or, finally, to consider leaving the situation.

WHAT YOU CAN DO TO MANAGE YOUR RESPONSE

- Identify the behaviour that bothers you

- Recognise that it is not your responsibility to change it

- Regularly practise one of the quick relaxation techniques in Chapter 7 to help stop an instant reaction

- Decide in advance how best you can respond to keep calm

- Refer back to the list of beliefs and find or create one to guide your inner voice

- Consider giving feedback using the guidelines in Chapter 8. Only do this if you are also prepared to receive feedback

---

People who make excessive demands on us can pile on the pressure. It is useful to develop the skills of saying 'no' for those circumstances in which we need to refuse requests or demands. To be able to do this we need to believe that it is acceptable for us to say 'no'. We also, if appropriate, need to show why this is a reasonable response.

Habits of always saying 'yes' can arise from a feeling that everyone else's needs are more important than ours. If this is the case, valuing our own needs and rights will require steady work – and by building stress fitness we are already moving in this direction. Interestingly, valuing ourselves and building self-esteem have the effect of generating respect from others. People will treat us as well as we expect to be treated, and as well as we treat ourselves. Saying 'no' is an important part of this process.

SAYING 'NO'

WHAT YOU CAN DO TO SAY 'NO'	
DO:	Listen carefully to the request
	Think about whether you will refuse or agree to it
	Recognise that you have a choice
	Say 'no' clearly and calmly if you choose to
	Explain your reasons
	Refuse the request, not the person
DON'T:	Apologise for saying 'no'
	Ask for approval or forgiveness
	Give excuses
	Say 'no' in words and 'yes' with your voice and body

TIME FOR STRESS

Time, and the demands placed on it both from our commitments and from ourselves, can be a vital element in stress.

How we spend our time may well cause us under- or overstress in the long term. The person who devotes all of his time to work at the expense of the rest of his life and is too exhausted at the end of the day to do anything of interest in the evening or at weekends, or the one who tries to cram so much into her life that she ends up overloaded and overstressed, are common examples. Between these extremes are endless variations of time problems leading to the sort of stress we do not want.

Feeling that we have insufficient time to do all that we want or need to do is a frequent pressure, often leading to home/work conflict, or causing dissatisfaction or frustration in the workplace. By contrast, spending time on tasks in which we have no interest may generate understress.

Effective time management is therefore an important part of stress management. It is not just about being more organised, although it does require discipline and commitment, for we are the only ones who can do it. Deciding to make changes to our use of time will mean different demands for a while, and people often say they don't have the time to work at it or to practise any stress management techniques. However, it is worth considering that we do not have the time not to! By working on time management we can often either remove or minimise the pressures of overstress, or progress up the Steps of understress, thus keeping ourselves healthily stressed.

Time management involves addressing three elements:

Goal clarification

Forward planning
and organisation

Making effective use of
time at the time

We need to be clear about our goals, plan to move smoothly towards them and use the time in the most effective way at the time. One of the goals can be that of managing our stress. Goal-setting and prioritising are covered in detail in Chapter 7.

WHAT YOU CAN DO TO BEGIN TIME MANAGEMENT

- Ask yourself: Am I satisfied with my time management?

- If the answer is 'no', make sure you read Chapters 6 and 7

TAKING TIME OUT

In a very busy life it is easy to be so caught up with responding to the demands that we do not take time out to reflect and review, to relax and recharge. Stepping back from a situation and allowing ourselves time to view it with clarity and consider our actions helps stop our progress towards the Spiral, and will help us manage the response.

Recharging our batteries, through relaxation and other activities, is an essential part of stress fitness. Lots of ways to train for stress fitness are suggested in Chapter 7.

DASHER OR STROLLER

How we go about our daily lives often reveals consistent patterns of behaviour and can give some clues about our levels and tolerance of stress. Most of us could describe someone we know who is always in a rush, impatient and hardly ever still – the Dasher. Then there is the person who never seems to be in a hurry, is rarely worried about deadlines and has a calm manner – the Stroller.

It is not always the Dasher, however, who will meet the deadline or be effective in the long run. It has been shown that those who behave like Dashers all the time are more likely to have heart attacks, so it could be worth while considering a change in behaviour. In spite of the Stroller's laid back manner, this person is often efficient and is considered to have a better chance of living to a ripe old age.

By looking at the two extremes in the checklist (adapted from Rosenman and Friedman, 1975) we may be able to see the side we identify with most. There may be differences in our behaviour at work and at home, or at different times or in different situations. These are not unalterable personality traits; they are habits of behaviour.

CHECKLIST	
Dasher	**Stroller**
Never late	Casual about time
Very competitive	Not competitive
Anticipates what others are going to say and finishes it for them	Listens well
Always feels rushed	Never feels rushed even under pressure
Impatient about waiting	Never impatient about waiting
Tries to do too many things at once	Takes things one at a time
Speaks emphatically and fast	Speaks slowly and deliberately

Wants public recognition at work	Personal satisfaction more important than what others think
Walks and eats fast	Does things slowly
Drives self and others hard	Easy going
Hides feelings	Shows feelings
Few outside interests	Many outside interests
Ambitious	Not ambitious
Eager to get things done	Casual

Dasher or Stroller behaviour may be appropriate at different times, so one behaviour is not necessarily healthier than the other in every circumstance. However, if we behave like a Dasher all the time it is unlikely that we will be building our stress fitness and we may well be spreading the stress virus. It is certainly possible, even if sometimes initially difficult, to change behaviour and move towards a Stroller style, if we want to. By choosing one or two of the areas and modifying our behaviour gradually we are likely to feel more relaxed and stress fit.

Difficulties can arise though if our organisation is impressed by people who dash about appearing to be businesslike and efficient. Much of this energy is often wasted. It is a sad fact that many of us wait until a heart attack or other illness forces us to pay attention and make the effort to change. We will listen to a doctor when we are already ill, but until that time we go on thinking it can never happen to us.

Example: Maurice

Maurice was a manager in a financial services company that encouraged all staff to be ambitious. He was determined to reach senior management, so he worked very hard, did a lot of overtime, took work home and never took his holiday entitlement. He was getting good annual appraisals and his work was noticed since he was bringing in new business.

He regularly worked through his lunchbreak so that he was available to his customers and was so tired when he got home that he never had the energy to go out in the evenings.

He was astonished when he began to get really bad nights during which he hardly slept, his mind going over and over the things that had happened during the day. He kept on reviewing his work, thinking of things he could have done better or opportunities he should have followed up. Consequently he ended up tired at the beginning of the morning and had to push himself to complete everything.

The pattern continued until he began to make mistakes. Concern about the deteriorating quality of his work meant he eventually dreaded going to work. There came a point, just before he reached the brink of the Spiral, when he went to his doctor to see if he could prescribe something to keep him going. The doctor recognised what was happening and gave him a copy of this book, which helped him to realise how he could remain effective but still find time to look after his whole self!

WHAT YOU CAN DO TO MODIFY DASHER BEHAVIOUR

● If you come out very near the Dasher column on any of the items, try to modify that particular behaviour, even in small ways to begin with that are consistent with still functioning effectively. For example, slow your walking and eating rate

● Tackle things in a steady way

● If you have to wait, use the time constructively

● Learn to relax, using the tips in Chapter 7

CHANGING THE PICTURE

Just as we develop habits of behaviour, so we tend to develop habits of perception. Understanding the way we see things, whilst difficult, is the first step in helping us to have some choices in the way we view any new situation. The next step is to generate skills to change the way we see stressful situations – particularly useful in those we cannot change.

You have an important meeting to attend and are stuck in a long tailback on the motorway. Your car phone has been returned for repairs, and you have no way of letting your client know why you are delayed. It is a crucial meeting with an important client who has already proved a difficult character. Central to your response is your view or perception of the situation:

FOR EXAMPLE: ON THE
MOTORWAY

Do you see it as threatening? Do you experience unhealthy stress? When you eventually arrive are you uptight and tense? Or do you keep calm, switch on your radio and enjoy the play, or put in your language cassette and catch up on your study, arriving apologetic yet relaxed?

Thoughts will go through your mind as you read the situation. These will combine with feelings you have about being late. Together these thoughts and feelings will affect and generate your behavioural response, which might well in itself create further feelings and thoughts. For example, if you are thinking, 'I can't be late – This is my most important client – She'll be furious I haven't called – I must get to a phone – My boss'll go crazy if we lose this one – Oh come on ... get a move on ...' anxiety will be building up and you will be feeling worried about the situation, feelings exacerbated by the recognition that you cannot change or control it.

Impatience, irritation or anger may well be generated. As your body goes into unhealthy stress response you may find yourself gripping the steering wheel, drumming your fingers on the dashboard, clenching your jaw and tensing your shoulders. Your breathing may well become shallow, your heart beat speed up. You may identify the feelings of discomfort that go with these changes, thus perhaps growing more anxious and concerned about the situation. And all the time the car is still stationary, or perhaps crawling along. You may then start trying to change the situation by lane-hopping, beeping your horn or frantically looking for a turn-off on the map. Thoughts, body, feelings and behaviour will all be involved.

The situation has generated these quite typical reactions of overstress. Your efforts to change the situation or influence the outcome are unlikely to be successful.

However, you do have some choices in all this. You CAN change the way you see the situation, you can change your thoughts and influence your feelings about it. As your perceptual habits will often have been learned, it is always possible to learn new ways of seeing things. This can help build up your stress fitness.

Think back to the motorway delay and the important meeting. Nothing in this situation has changed except your perception. Instead of the thoughts identified previously, you are now saying to yourself:

'This is an important meeting, but I can't change the situation.'

'I'll have to explain as clearly as possible when I get there and run the meeting really effectively.'

'It's no point me getting angry, it won't do any good.'

'How else could I use this time right now?'

'I must keep calm so that I get there in a fit state.'

'As soon as I can get off this motorway I'll call to explain. If necessary we'll have to reschedule the meeting.'

Taking control of our thoughts enables productive and rational ones to help generate feelings of calm. Practising one of the techniques in Chapter 7, such as deep breathing or quick relaxation, helps maintain the calmness. Essentially, changing thinking to change the perception manages the response. In this example the realisation of what can and cannot be changed allows a focus on what can be done about it.

WHAT YOU CAN DO TO CHANGE THE THOUGHTS

In a stressful situation you cannot change:

- Recognise the thoughts about the situation that are pushing you towards an unhealthy stress response

- Replace the negative thoughts with more helpful thoughts to enable you to cope with the situation

- Think of practical ways that could help to improve the situation later

- At the same time, practise one of the quick relaxation techniques from Chapter 7

Another method of altering the way we see a situation is to put it into a broader perspective. When we are up to our eyes in unhealthy stress, we can lose sight of what is important and the pressures can take on a huge significance, often greater than they merit. It does not help immediately to be told that others are worse off, or to consider world problems if we feel stressed. None the less, putting the pressures into some sort of personally significant perspective or fitting them into a scheme of things of what is important – relating to ourselves and a wider context – can have profound effects.

INTO PERSPECTIVE

LETTING GO

As we have seen, some of the most stressful times are those where we have no control over what is happening. We can do ourselves a lot of harm by stewing over a problem endlessly and working ourselves up into a state of helpless fury. Feelings that we should change the situation, or that it should not be happening at all, are equally unhelpful. This puts us straight into overstress and we might feel our blood pressure rising, heart pumping and hands sweating.

When faced with a seemingly impossible situation, whether it is one that has built up over a period of time or a temporary irritating incident, there are always choices we can make.

Example: Steve and Frances

The chief executive of a small manufacturing firm in an area of high unemployment decided that working hours should be changed from 9–5 to 8–4 so that suppliers could deliver early in the day, avoiding the rush hour. Steve went round grumbling and talking to all his mates about it and how unfair it was. Frances sounded out the others about whether it was making difficulties for them in seeing their children to school in the morning, as it was for her. She then organised a deputation to the chief executive to try to change her mind.

Not only was Steve spending a lot of time and energy in grumbling to everyone, but he was also spreading the stress virus and feeding into people's feelings of powerlessness so that morale was being affected. Frances, on the other hand, was using her frustration more constructively to try to change the situation that had been created. Even though she was not able to get the chief executive to change her mind, she did at least feel that she had given it a go. Then she spent her time helping to organise a rota for seeing children to school.

Others in the firm had just decided that there was no point in making a fuss as they were afraid of losing their jobs. This might, in some cases, have led them to suffer from the kind of understress that took them along the short-cut to overstress, but some of them were able to shrug it off and get on with the job.

Several strategies may help to keep us in healthy stress at these times. The main point to consider is whether our habitual response is effective or whether we are wasting a lot of energy that could be used in more constructive ways.

First, we need to assess the situation and decide if there is something we can do to influence it – in which case we should take action. However, it is very important to recognise when no action is possible and there is absolutely nothing we can do. In these circumstances we should decide if it would be healthier to let it go.

Letting go is easier said than done, but, given the choice of overstress or staying effective, it is certainly wiser to let go of the pressure. As we learn more about stress and its effects on us, and develop stress fitness by practising the techniques outlined in this book, letting go becomes easier.

WHAT YOU CAN DO TO LET GO OF STRESS

- Step back from the situation

- Identify the pressure(s)

- Separate the reaction from the cause

- Clearly identify if personal action can change the situation or not

- Recognise that if no personal action can influence then letting go or worrying are the only options

- Understand the harm unhealthy stress can cause

- Remind yourself of how unhealthy stress helps no one

- Resolve to use thinking skills to stop worrying further

> - Use the inner voice to remind yourself of your stress rights
>
> - Decide not to react

Letting off steam somewhere appropriate and working off the energy in a healthy way are also helpful. Humour can often help here: a good laugh relieves tension and helps to put things in perspective. Talking about what is going on can also help remove some of the intensity.

INVEST IN ACTION

Certain situations carry the potential for great pressure, particularly if we are unused to them. These situations are often characterised by the requirement that we present ourselves to others, for example:

- a job interview

- a new job or work challenge

- meeting new people

- public speaking

Whilst we may well find that in such circumstances the stress we experience has the effect of raising our performance – to the Peaks – we may also be so affected by the fear that we suffer unhealthy stress. If we are to make the most of the stress we will need a strategy.

The most important thing is to anticipate the stress and prepare to meet it head on. Preparation is a vital tool and we will need to allow enough time for this, not only preparing practically for the event, but also tackling the thought patterns that lead us to unhealthy stress. In fact the former will help us in the latter.

We should find out as much as we can about the audience, the venue, the subject matter and the parameters of the talk. Then we should generate ideas, plan the outline and impose a structure on the talk, plan the talk in detail and then translate it into notes, perhaps using cue cards. The next stage is to practise our delivery, paying attention to use of voice and body language, including movement and gesture, facial expression

FOR EXAMPLE: A STRATEGY TO PREPARE FOR A FORMAL PRESENTATION

and eye contact with the audience. We should mark our notes as appropriate to remind us when to pause, slow down, smile, and so on. Having done all this, timed our talk and practised speaking from notes and responding to questions if we expect them, then we can tackle the nerves.

One of the effects of planning in this way is to reduce anxiety because we are thoroughly prepared. We have made sure that our performance will benefit from as much preliminary work as is possible and this will raise our confidence level. In fact low confidence often arises from feeling unskilled for the task.

However, low confidence also often stems from thoughts of failure, believing that we are bound to make a mess of it, and the negative view, even before we start, that it will not go well. This can prevent us from preparing, so we prove ourselves right! If we feel like this, we will be communicating anxiety and we will not give a confident performance.

The second aspect of preparation is to replace these thoughts with more positive and helpful ones, which encourage us to achieve. The important thing is to appear confident, even if it is only on the surface. People will then respond to us as if we are, since that is how they see us, which will have the effect of encouraging us to think we are confident. Behaviour can precede attitude; by behaving confidently we will eventually become so.

What will help us in the initial behaviour is to visualise ourselves in the situation, in this case giving the talk, but doing it effectively. This, coupled with the practical preparation we will also have completed, will support us in meeting the demands of the new and stressful situation.

TACKLE THE PROBLEM

In times of unhealthy stress one obvious – but sometimes overlooked – strategy is to confront whatever is causing the pressure and do something about it. Most importantly, though, we have to identify what really is the problem. We may feel that it is the work overload, but perhaps it is our inability to say 'no'. We might blame it all on a difficult colleague, but instead it is our own unremitting standards creating internal pressures. Once the cause of the pressures is clear, then a plan of action can be instigated.

It is interesting that often when under great pressure we know exactly what we need to do to help us through, yet we do not do it. For example, after an exhausting and demanding day at work, knowing that we should go swimming or to the gym, we slump in front of the television and eat chocolate, or go to the pub. It takes a huge effort of will to take the action needed when we feel like doing the opposite. We have to believe that it is worth doing on two counts: first, we can make an impact and our efforts will give results, and secondly, if not more importantly, we deserve it.

An awareness of the implications of not taking action can prove a motivating force. It is easier, however, when we schedule in stress management strategies, as detailed in Chapter 7, so that they become part of our routine and we do not have to make decisions about doing them – they happen automatically. Thus coping strategies become preventive techniques and regular attention to our stress builds stress fitness as if we were in training.

DO IT NOW!

6 *Working with Stress*

WORK NEEDS

A range of needs are met by working. The MORI report, *Blueprint for Success* (Webb, 1989), the result of a survey involving employees in Britain in 1989, showed that the first four reasons that people gave for working were, in order of importance:

1 having an interesting and enjoyable job,
2 job security,
3 the feeling of accomplishing something worthwhile,
4 basic pay.

Over time, changing interests, concerns, priorities and expectations can affect what we put into and expect from work. Accepting that this is normal development can help us to keep in touch with the changes.

Example: Rosalynn

Rosalynn had spent ten years working at home, bringing up her children and supporting her partner who was the main wage-earner. Since her children had been at school she had found many interests to occupy her and was always busy in some sporting, creative or social pursuit that filled her 'spare' time. However, she had been becoming increasingly lethargic and miserable and, unable to fathom out why, she had embarked on a course to explore options in the workplace for women returners. It was then that she realised that her work needs, for a sense of purpose and for variety and stimulation, were not being met: in effect she was understressed and needed to return to paid work that challenged her.

If needs are not being met at work this can create pressure. For instance, if we like variety in our work and have been moved to more repetitive jobs then our needs are not being met. The change is acting as a constraint, without providing support, so we will suffer from understress. At the other extreme, if we are given several projects on subjects in which we are not interested and which require a great deal of concentration for a long time, we shall have so much work that we do not enjoy that we will become overstressed and less effective. What we personally need are jobs that, over all, support our need for variety and therefore keep us working in the Peaks.

Example: Malcolm

As a technician in a laboratory Malcolm generally worked alone on specific, short-term projects, liaising with his team leader for direction and with his colleagues for problem-solving, advice and exchange of information. Proficient at his job, he was pleased to be promoted to a supervisory position in a more fast-moving department. In this new role he was responding to requests and demands from customers, both internal and external. He supervised the work of a shift team and had his first experience of management.

Initially the constant demands of others seemed rather intrusive, if reasonably simple to deal with. However, as time went on, he found himself actively resenting the interruptions to his own work schedule, and wondering when he would find time for his own projects, which he insisted on keeping as the most senior team member. He became more short-tempered and irritable with his team and, when the work pace went up a gear with a new contract, he found he was making elementary errors in his own work.

A management course led him to reassess his role in the team and recognise that his job was to coordinate the work of others. However, his strong preference was for a solitary and technical type of work. He found the nature of his new role, with its reactive, people-management focus, strongly at odds with his work preferences and this was causing him overstress.

An important step in stress management is to understand our work needs at each stage of our lives and to recognise when they are not being met. With this knowledge it is sometimes possible to take action to remedy the situation. Where changes have been imposed from outside, in which no action is possible, we must acknowledge the under- or overstress and build up supports to help us to cope.

WHAT YOU CAN DO TO IDENTIFY YOUR WORK NEEDS

Opposite are examples of work needs.

● Identify which you have now by ticking the name box

● Then consider whether these are being fulfilled or not in your present situation, and tick or cross the box under each of your needs

● For those needs that are not being fulfilled, consider:

 – What stops them being met? (Constraints)
 – What would enable them to be met? (Supports)
 – What action could you take to maximise the supports and minimise the constraints?
 – If no action is possible, what can you do to help yourself through this period? See Chapter 7

HOME/WORK CONFLICT

How many times have difficulties arisen when two partners, both with demanding jobs, have found that childcare arrangements have broken down and one of the children is sick? Or when an anniversary celebration has been planned months in advance and the chief executive insists on a late meeting? Or when an elderly relative needs extra care and support? We can feel we are being torn in two by such divided loyalties.

Although stereotypically men have put their jobs first in this type of situation, both partners now often have similar

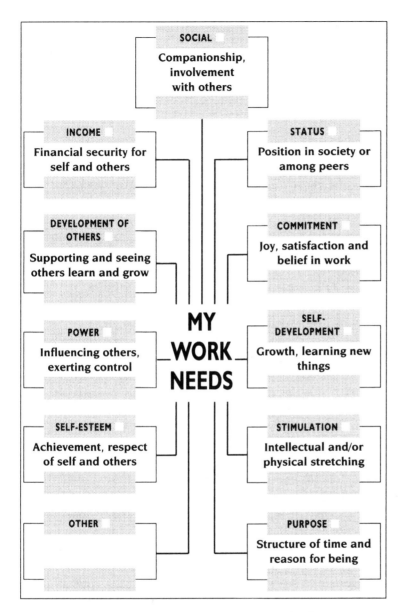

SOCIAL
Companionship, involvement with others

INCOME
Financial security for self and others

STATUS
Position in society or among peers

DEVELOPMENT OF OTHERS
Supporting and seeing others learn and grow

COMMITMENT
Joy, satisfaction and belief in work

POWER
Influencing others, exerting control

MY WORK NEEDS

SELF-DEVELOPMENT
Growth, learning new things

SELF-ESTEEM
Achievement, respect of self and others

STIMULATION
Intellectual and/or physical stretching

OTHER

PURPOSE
Structure of time and reason for being

demands at work and at home. Both sexes are also beginning to see that the costs of focusing on only one aspect of life are not always worth it, in terms of health, social life and other interests.

Some of the main areas of home/work conflict that may lead to overstress are:

● feeling guilty about not being at home to look after the children

- resenting not spending enough time with the family

- missing out on social life because of working extremely long hours

- the demands of dependent relatives conflicting with work responsibilities

- not earning enough to meet expenses or to satisfy a preferred lifestyle

- expecting to fulfil two roles, at home and at work, to perfection

There are signs that people are beginning to think seriously about improving how work is organised to make life less stressful for both men and women. There is also evidence that some of the assumptions made in the past about the relationship between our working lives and our home lives are being challenged. If new, flexible ways can be found of managing a reasonable balance between the two, then a large area of overstress could be reduced.

For example, in Britain, we tend to work excessively long hours. A study by the Low Pay Unit (1992) discovered that British male workers work 4.5 hours longer each week than their European counterparts, with one in eight working longer than the maximum 48 hours a week recommended by the EEC. Whilst the leaner organisation, towards which most organisations are currently aiming, is partly the cause, British culture associates long hours with commitment and achievement. In a radio broadcast, Sir John Harvey Jones has described it as 'this appalling British habit ... often seen as a sign of virility'. Cary Cooper considers the potential damage caused to family and performance by long working hours. He suggests that there is research evidence that the optimal working week is 35–45 hours (Cooper and Sutherland, 1992).

Only the Americans and the Japanese apparently work longer hours than the British. However, karoshi or 'death by overwork' is causing concern in Tokyo and research in America identifies that most heart attacks occur at 9 o'clock on Monday morning.

By challenging the cultural expectation that long hours are essential for success, we could not only reduce home/work conflict and the dangers of overstress, but also free time that could be used to build up stress fitness. We need to evaluate our performance against output, not hours worked.

LIVING TO WORK OR WORKING TO LIVE?

The concept of stress fitness means that we must look at the place of work within the total life picture. It is rare to find that all our needs can be met in just one of our roles. Those who try this run the risk of having no needs met if their situations should change dramatically.

Paid work quite often seems to require total attention and commitment, which can lead to our neglecting other aspects of our lives such as family, health and friends. Without minimising the need to earn a living and to work effectively, it is helpful to identify how much of ourselves we give to our jobs and whether we are happy with that in the context of other important areas of our lives. We may be using some skills, abilities or talents in one role but others in different roles. If we look at our lives as a whole we have a better chance of fulfilling our potential overall and maintaining a balance of activity that can keep us stress fit.

WORK/HOME BALANCE

Example: Paul

Paul had always been totally committed to his work in advertising. He enjoyed the excitement of working creatively to tight deadlines. He perceived the need to keep abreast of changes in the industry and recognised that, to be successful, he had to put in long hours both at work and at related social functions. This was fine until he and his partner had children.

His previous work pattern did not fit in with his role as father – to which he both wanted and needed to devote regular time. Failure to spend time at business functions meant he was not maintaining contacts that were needed for his own progress and to complete team tasks. By neglecting these he would be jeopardising his long-term success, more important now with a family to support. Paul was suffering from overstress because his situation had changed over time and it was becoming impossible to satisfy both his work and home needs.

One way of working out how much time we spend on work as a proportion of the rest of our lives is to draw a pie-chart that represents a week or a month (excluding sleep, unless this is an issue for you). It might look something like this:

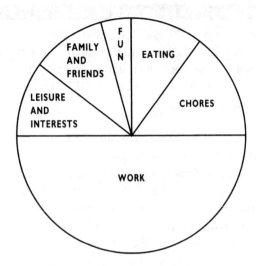

The time pie

What each of us needs to decide is whether we have the segments in the right proportion for us at the moment. Is enough support represented there? If not, what are the constraints preventing us from putting it right and what can we do about it?

WHAT YOU CAN DO TO ASSESS THE ROLE OF WORK IN YOUR LIFE

- Make a pie-chart of your own life, choosing your own categories. Mark the slices as they seem to you

- Is work the largest slice of your life around which you structure most other things?

- Is this ok?

- Are you allowing time for the things that are important to you?

- Are you expecting all your needs to be met by just one aspect of your life?

- Do you need to move towards more equal-sized slices?

- Would you enjoy a different relationship with work in the future?

- If so, can you take steps to move towards it? (Because our feelings will sometimes affect how we see things, it would be worth while keeping an accurate record, over a limited period of time, of what time you really do spend in each of the slices. See if it is different from what you thought.)

- Now repeat the exercise, but this time divide the pie how you would like it to be

- What are the differences?

- What are you going to do about it?

- Chapter 7 might help you

CHANGING CAREERS

Stereotypes and views of career paths can conflict with our experience of reality. The causes of dissatisfaction with our working lives may be difficult to pinpoint but, if we feel that the picture is not unfolding as it should, then further confusion can blind us to the actions we need to take.

Wanting some satisfaction from our careers is natural. What is not so natural is the expectation that satisfaction can be achieved without thought and effort. We need to examine our assumptions about work and careers, and be clear about our attitudes towards accepting responsibility and taking control over what we do.

First we must consider the way that career paths and working patterns are changing. It seems that, instead of predominantly working in one area or field, and for one organisation, all their lives, people increasingly expect to:

- change jobs frequently
- change careers at least once
- be self-employed for some years at least
- engage in other activities such as studying, doing voluntary work and working at home for part of their lives

Charles Handy, in *The Age of Unreason* (1989), describes the work portfolio as made up of wage or fee work (paid), home work, gift work and study work. 'Home' work encompasses everything to do with the home and family; 'gift' work is that which we do voluntarily, and 'study' work is self-development and learning. Handy sees this as increasingly the pattern of our lives. Such a portfolio not only enables our varying needs at different times to be met, thus reducing unhealthy stress, but it also allows us to put work into perspective in our lives. Similarly, and of course relatedly, it reflects the changing structure of organisations. With social change and economic development or recession, companies will continue to change the methods they use to employ people. One way is to rely on a core staff for essential tasks and to call in consultants, independents and associates on short-term and fee-earning contracts when other work is needed and available. These practices mean changes in traditional career paths, away from the 'one job' or 'one organisation' approach.

Example: Anna

Anna worked as a teacher of sociology and economics in a further education college. She had always enjoyed the variety intrinsic in teaching different groups of students and was never bored with her job. However, after ten years progressing steadily through the teaching grades she began to question her career path. Although she loved her work, she had been feeling unsettled and unenthusiastic about another academic year. She was reluctant to take on a more senior management role, feeling that it would not be stimulating enough: she knew she could run a large faculty successfully but she needed a different sort of challenge. She began to consider a career change and, after extensive self-assessment and careers advice, she identified that research would offer her a new beginning. She began by working voluntarily for a local pressure group and work-shadowing a television researcher. Eventually she secured a temporary contract researching for a documentary programme, which she completed in her vacation. When she applied for a permanent job her experience and commitment meant she was successful.

In her new career she found the constant challenge of using her skills on short-term projects, travelling to different locations and working with new people met her stress needs more appropriately at that point in her career.

As women progress up the career ladder and gain greater influence in organisations, the issue of home/work balance, which women have always debated, becomes mainstream. As women face greater choices in their lives, and challenge traditional career paths and definitions of success, the next development seems to be that men are questioning the priorities in their lives. Cary Cooper's research (Cooper and Sutherland, 1992) among chief executives in Europe reveals dissatisfaction with the pressures of an executive lifestyle. He found that large numbers of people were actively thinking of quitting and were expressing a strong desire to attain some sort of balance between home and work. As men question their commitment and effort at work, the family is becoming a crunch issue.

Opportunities within organisations and, as a result, career paths are undergoing fundamental changes because of these developments. As has already been discussed, change is itself a creator of pressure, in this case exacerbated by confrontation with a situation for which we may be unprepared. We must therefore take a fresh look at careers. A practical view of a career is that it is a series of purposeful activities, each one equally valuable, which taken together make a whole. Joanna Foster, chair of the Equal Opportunities Commission, speaks of the 'patchwork' career, which expresses the concept clearly, sharing some of the focus of the 'portfolio' career.

If we are to minimise unhealthy stress connected with our careers we need to take some control over our career paths so that they enhance our lives. This means building up our skills and keeping a watch on how our own development is progressing.

CAREER STAGES

Particular pressures tend to happen at certain times in our careers. They can cause overstress if we are not stress fit, or if constraints in our lives outweigh the supports. The pressures described in the following pages do not necessarily belong to only one stage. But we need to be aware of them in ourselves as much as in people who work with or for us.

EARLY WORK LIFE

Our first work will be the jobs that we are expected to do at home, and perhaps weekend or holiday jobs, where we begin to understand that we will be expected to be reliable and be on time. We will probably still be supported by family and friends.

When we take on our first 'real' job, however, we will be more on our own and may well find pressure coming from:

– wondering if we shall be able to cope
– not knowing the other people
– not knowing our way around
– travelling to work
– being restricted by work times
– developing personal relationships
– learning new skills
– perhaps living away from home for the first time

All these can be exciting, particularly taking charge of our own destinies. Induction programmes, if provided, help to relieve some of the pressures of a new environment.

Example: Mike

Mike had begun a job in a government office and was living away from home for the first time. He felt very lucky to have got the job and his family were pleased for him. A few months after he arrived his boss noticed that he was beginning to withdraw and was losing enthusiasm for his work. She was puzzled because she had taken trouble to see that his induction had been thorough and she could not find out from him what the trouble was. Eventually she suggested that he have a word with the Welfare Officer as he might be able to help.

The Welfare Officer discovered that Mike was living in a hostel where there were no other young people. Mike was also finding work difficult, not helped by the fact that his immediate colleague was very much older and was impatient with him. He was afraid that if he told his boss she would see him as a 'wimp' and he would get a bad report, perhaps not passing his probationary period. He was keeping away from his family because he felt he was letting them down. With the help of the Welfare Officer Mike found himself new digs where there were other young workers and he also joined the office sports club. The Welfare Officer helped Mike to develop his assertive skills so that he could cope with his colleague better, letting her know how her impatience affected him and how she could really help him.

As a result Mike's boss was able to recommend him for a permanent post when the time came.

During this stage we are beginning to know ourselves better, as well as perhaps changing jobs or organisations. We will be maturing by learning to manage ourselves at home and at work so there will be other pressures:

DEVELOPING WORK LIFE

- taking on new responsibilities
- promotion
- more travel
- a change of career
- further study or learning
- coping with changes in the organisation
- moving into a new post or organisation
- moving home
- our partner's expectations conflicting with our own
- establishing a family
- divorce, remarriage, step-children
- work breaks for work or family reasons
- financial commitments
- redundancy

The potential for overloading ourselves at this stage is very high, particularly if we are ambitious. Instances of home/work conflict are likely to be frequent unless we keep a watchful eye on the balance between them. We need to pay special attention to our stress fitness at this time so that we do not run the risk of going over the edge onto the Spiral.

This can be the stage when we have achieved what we want and are enjoying the results of previous effort. On the other hand, it can be the time when we recognise that we are not going to achieve what we had hoped for; we are perhaps having to tolerate a work situation that is far from ideal. Pressures here may include all those from the previous stage as well as:

ESTABLISHED WORK LIFE

- second or third career
- conflict between where we want to be and where our organisation expects us to be
- recognition that some hopes will not be fulfilled
- children becoming more expensive
- children leaving home

– partner taking on a new career
– parents ageing and needing more care
– younger people threatening our position
– introduction of new technology
– redundancy or early retirement

Even more care needs to be taken here to acknowledge the issues and find strategies for dealing with them constructively. The physical aspects of our lives may need special attention, particularly if we are involved in business entertaining and have sedentary jobs.

LATER WORK LIFE

In this stage we could be comfortable in every way and feeling very satisfied with how our career has gone. We may be in a position of influence and be fulfilling our potential, meeting enormous challenges with great skill. On the other hand, we may be functioning not very well, with reduced supplies of energy and struggling to survive in what seems like a hostile environment. If we are losing some of our abilities and skills, on which we prided ourselves, this can have a bad effect on how we feel about ourselves. Pressures that are more likely to apply in this stage are:

– heavy responsibilities with less energy for them
– a run-down of responsibilities, which leaves us either relieved or regretful – either way a change
– redundancy, early retirement or retirement itself
– a partner retiring
– becoming the older generation
– becoming a grandparent
– friends and family dying
– not being able to do the things we used to do
– other people doing things for us

If we do not come to terms with some of these changes, we will not give ourselves the chance to plan a really satisfying retirement. We need to be aware of the need to build in some healthy stress to keep us fit but without overloading ourselves unnecessarily.

Example: Sue
Sue had brought up a family who were now all leading their own lives. She had divorced her husband and was

living with a new partner who had retired before her. She was filled with foreboding at the thought of her imminent retirement from the hospital where she was a sister. She was becoming quite depressed at the thought of not working any more and meeting people on a regular basis. She suddenly realised that one of the problems was the thought of being at home with her partner all day and night, even though they loved each other very much. She recognised that she would have to make sure that she and her partner had different interests to occupy them, at least part of the time, after she had given up paid work. In the end she was able to train to become a tutor on the adult basic education course and her partner was able to follow a life-long interest in local history.

Throughout our lives we shall probably strike patches of overstress and understress, as this is the way we learn to cope. With the help of understanding how we react to the pressures and what we can do to help ourselves, we stand a good chance of leading a reasonably balanced life.

WHAT YOU CAN DO ABOUT UNHEALTHY STRESS IN CAREER STAGES

- Take stock of your objectives in life regularly

- When doing this, include your objectives for outside work

- Work out your priorities at each stage with the other people close to you

- Make sure that you are building in a balance that will enhance your stress fitness

---

HIGH PRESSURE POINTS

It is unlikely that we will go through our working lives without some experience of personal crises causing acute pressure for a while. Many people sail through and rebuild their lives very positively; they are likely to have constructive attitudes but will also have enough support, of various kinds, around them. Those who have real difficulty in readjusting will probably have less support around and there will be real dangers of suffering from unhealthy stress. Also involved are gains and losses, opportunities and dangers (either real or perceived). Initially we may not be able to see the gains or opportunities clearly because we are coping with the shock of change.

As we have seen in Chapter 3, there is likely to be overstress around change, particularly if it is unexpected. We will need to find some means to deal with this if we are to work through the experience and restore a healthy balance afterwards. What often happens is that feelings are suppressed and burst out at inappropriate times, sometimes being translated into endless blaming, or we get locked into other unconstructive patterns of behaviour that prevent us from reorganising our lives in the best way we can in the circumstances.

Even if the changes are welcome, there will still be a need for adjustment and this can cause pressure. However, if we find ways of managing those pressures and can use the energy to create something positive out of the situation, then we will have learned how to survive healthily and this will leave us more stress fit for any future crises. We can look at it as becoming immunised against the dangers of unhealthy stress.

PROMOTION

Promotion can offer a real boost to morale and new opportunities, but it also entails new responsibilities involving new relationships, new work patterns, possible relocation and loss of familiar support.

TAKE-OVERS AND MERGERS

The upheavals usually associated with these events cause great uncertainty and anxiety about jobs. Once they know the worst, people often show great resilience, but the repercussions will probably still leave them with a strong dose of overstress.

DEMOTION AND DISMISSAL

The loss of status and money involved in demotion and dismissal can affect people profoundly, particularly because of the change of role. The consequences for relationships and financial commitments can be very far-reaching and it is difficult for people to readjust quickly after either of these experiences.

REDUNDANCY

There are similarities between redundancy and demotion or dismissal as they all involve a change of role and, probably, lifestyle.

These may be provoked by any of the above events, but they are increasingly being chosen by people who find that they are not being fulfilled in their present occupation. While some people may now have several careers in a life-time, each time the changes will create pressures.

CAREER CHANGES

The reasons for taking work breaks are many: further training or study, sabbaticals, family commitments or travel are some of the more common. If the intention is to return to the same organisation, there is likely to be some uncertainty, perhaps about seniority or whether there will be a job to return to at all.

Some people find that the experience of taking a break to look after small children leaves them with feelings of low self-esteem and of being undervalued. They may have chosen willingly to do the job, which involves skilled and valuable work, and find great satisfaction in it. At the same time, they can feel that they have little power or control over their lives, which lowers their self-confidence.

It is sometimes thought that, from a work point of view, a break to bring up a family is a waste of time. This ignores the valuable management skills that have probably been exercised and developed, like dealing with several demands at the same time, managing time flexibly, cooperating with others and organising activities. The insight into child development and parenting can also be particularly helpful in some professions.

Lack of recognition of these factors, both at home and at work, can lead to particularly low confidence levels when returning to paid work.

WORK BREAKS

The frustration of people who cannot understand why they are not being promoted when there is no obvious reason can cause an enormous amount of pressure on those who are ambitious. It may be because of their gender, race, colour, creed or simply that those in control think that they do not 'fit'. Because the barriers are hidden it can be very difficult to confront the real issues, and they are sometimes referred to as 'glass ceilings'.

INVISIBLE BARRIERS

More people than ever before are being offered early retirement. For those who still feel that they want to go on working it can be extremely frustrating, particularly if it seems that the reasons are financial, because younger people can be paid less. For many it is a welcome release, but even this

EARLY RETIREMENT

involves a great readjustment earlier than expected.

RETIREMENT

Although most people are forced to retire at some stage in their careers, the complete change of lifestyle can come as a shock unless good preparation has been made. The loss of status, activity and income can lead to a loss of self-esteem and feelings of not being wanted any more, which can progress into depression.

RELOCATION

Many people are relocated as part of their career development but it can also happen as a result of any of the events already mentioned above. Research by Dr Munton for the Medical Research Council (1991) found that the stress resulting from relocation could have far-reaching effects on mental health, family relationships and effectiveness at work. The circumstances of the person involved will be extremely important in determining whether there will be a high degree of overstress or not. A partner with a career, children at school, support networks and other factors will all influence how the person will be able to cope.

Example: Andrew and Jane

Andrew and Jane were moving house because Andrew's promotion meant leaving a small town, branch office to work at head office. Andrew was delighted because he would be doing more interesting work; he felt he was moving up in the world and they would be able to afford a better house. Although she was unhappy about moving, Jane felt she had no choice, not wanting to hinder Andrew's promotion. She enjoyed her part-time job, which could have led to further opportunities as the children grew up. All she could see was what she was going to lose in the way of work, friends, relations who lived near, childcare networks and a pleasant lifestyle. She was also worried about resettling the children in new schools, but Andrew kept saying that other children coped and so would theirs. It was not surprising that they began to have real difficulties in their relationship, which just added to the pressures.

When several of these things happen within months of each other, then the levels of stress will be very high. A recognition of this fact can often help us to understand why it is that we do

not feel we are coping well, when we expected to. This is
particularly true when we are promoted and decide to move
house; or when we retire and decide to move to a different part
of the country. For most of us it is helpful to leave time to
readjust to one change before we undertake another, but some
of us, with a high tolerance of pressures, will thrive on constant
change.

When we are experiencing any of these high pressure points
it is extremely important to read and take action on the ideas
put forward in Chapter 7.

**WHAT YOU CAN DO TO HELP WITH HIGH PRESSURE
POINTS**

- Gather as much information as possible

- Develop extra support strategies to help yourself
  during this time (see Chapter 7)

- Try to think positively about the best options

- Set yourself some goals and an action plan

- Work on your emotional responses. Allow yourself to
  express your feelings where appropriate

- Be clear about what you can and cannot change

- Work on looking for the opportunities that high
  pressure points may offer

---

7 The Balancing Act

By its very nature balance is elusive, and in active lives absolute equilibrium can be held for only fleeting moments. To manage our stress effectively we need to strive for an overall balance between the different elements of our lives. This means that, although we may be climbing the Steps, tackling the Peaks or trying to pull ourselves back out of the Spiral, we are taking regular action to keep stress fit.

It is therefore necessary to be alert to the elements that contribute to balance and to have a strategy for maintaining us in the process of balancing. Regularly taking action to build stress fitness needs to become part of the routine of living. This chapter gives some ideas about how this can be done. At times when the pressure is really on we need to pay more – not less – attention to those activities that support us.

The Industrial Society survey showed that many organisations are recognising the value of fitness for work by providing occupational health services, training in relaxation techniques and stress management, sporting facilities and physical fitness clinics, social clubs, counselling and other ways for people to work through difficulties in their lives. Investment in the welfare of employees can be rationalised by the return; people will be more effective in their work. It is perhaps more important that we should make sure that, in our own lives, we pay attention to our own stress fitness.

WHAT YOU CAN DO TO BEGIN MONITORING YOUR STRESS FITNESS

Mark against each of these statements:

    R – regularly

    S – sometimes

    N – never

- I manage the time I spend on the different parts of my life satisfactorily

- I meet people with whom I can talk

- I have at least one close friend in whom I can confide

- I am able to express my feelings

- I give and receive affection

- I keep a check on tensions in my body and have ways of reducing them

- I make sure I do something that relaxes me after a stressful time

- I take a quiet time for myself at least once a day

- I laugh and have fun

- I walk, rather than drive or ride, whenever possible

- I use the stairs rather than a lift when practicable

- I take reasonably energetic exercise at least twice a week

- I choose TV or radio programmes, or books or magazines that interest me

- I have an absorbing interest or hobby apart from work

- I am clear about my sense of values and what is important in my life

- I am the appropriate weight for my age, height and build

- I eat at least one balanced meal a day

- I limit my drinks of tea, coffee, chocolate and cola to three or less a day

cont.

- I keep within the recommended limits for alcohol of 21 units (men) or 14 units (women), spread over a week

- I give myself treats

Now see how many R's, S's and N's there are. If there are 17 or more R's and S's then you are probably pretty stress fit. If there are more than 5 N's then you need to do something to make them S's or R's

STRESS HEALTH

There is a lingering puritanical feeling in many of us that if we are having fun and doing something that stimulates us pleasurably then we are wasting time. In fact, we are helping to keep ourselves healthy in every sense. Unless we manage some degree of balance, we will not be effective people in any part of our lives.

The three types of stress experience each need a slightly different approach.

UNDERSTRESS

If work is dull and repetitive, then we need to find things to do outside work that develop our skills and interests. If our lifestyle is dull, then perhaps work can compensate by providing more challenges to keep us functioning well. As we probably have more control over our own time outside work this is where we can have more influence.

Example: Jim

Jim had played a lot of basketball at school but had let it drop when he first went to work. His job was a sedentary one in an office where he was constantly having to meet deadlines. He began to realise that he was not feeling particularly bright in the mornings, which wasn't like him, so he found out where there was a basketball club and joined. Even though it took an effort to get home and change after a day's work, he felt much better in himself and found that he was able to think more clearly at work.

When we are frustrated by understress, finding constructive ways of dispersing the pent-up energy will be useful. But when we begin to climb the Steps it is important to prepare for the pressures ahead. By doing this we will have a better chance of retaining some balance, even if there are unexpected crises. Strategies that become part of our living routines will stand us in good stead when the pressures really build up.

If the demands that are being made on us mean that we have less energy and time for the balancing activities, there is a danger that we may let them slide or put them lower on our list of priorities. However, the process of keeping up with interests outside work will help us to maintain a state of stress fitness through the Peaks.

Example: Carol

Carol has a busy life running a home and working freelance, so she has very irregular hours of work. She found she was not able to sing in the choir she had joined because they had a regular evening for rehearsals which she was often not able to get to. So she has joined a small group of singers who meet more irregularly to suit the members. Some evenings she has to drag herself out to rehearsals but finds that each time she comes back reinvigorated. She reckons that this is partly due to the enjoyable company with a shared interest, but also because she has to breathe more deeply than during her normal life and she gets great emotional satisfaction from the music.

Too often we keep going at a fierce pace and are surprised when we come to the end of our tether, suffer burn-out or become quite seriously ill. Once on the Spiral, restoring some measure of balance and stress fitness is more difficult but more vital.

A complete review of our lifestyle can help to pin-point areas that need attention. Too often what we could have done to look after ourselves in the first place has to be done in hospital or on doctor's orders.

Example: Trevor

Trevor was a very successful chief executive of a medium-sized business. He loved his work and travelled extensively between the various sites of the organisation. He spent very little time with his family and this built up tensions between him and his wife, as he rarely spent time with the children since he was always too tired when he came home. He used to play golf but gave it up because his wife was fed up with him being out at the weekends too.

To his amazement, at the firm's regular health check-up the doctor detected some heart trouble. Trevor continued to work at the same pace and the trouble got worse. With the doctor's help he had a radical rethink about his lifestyle and found that he was able to delegate more work than before, leaving more time in the evenings for his family. He was even able to persuade some of his family to take up golf and, by spending more time together, the atmosphere at home improved.

The feeling that we should not 'fuss' over ourselves, or that we are being selfish if we put ourselves first, is common. While there needs to be a balance between our needs and those of other people, if we never put ourselves first, and no one else does it for us, we are much more likely to suffer from unhealthy stress. This will be compounded by the feeling that we have no control over our lives. We often find it difficult to recognise our own, very significant, role in managing or not managing our own stress.

We are more likely to be useful members of the workplace, our families and society in general if we are in a state where we can deal with life effectively, and this implies looking after our stress fitness, not constantly sliding down the Spiral.

SUPPORT NETWORKS

One way in which we can begin to look after ourselves is by making sure that there are people around us who can help when we need someone else. How close we want to be to other people will vary, but, in terms of having a balance in our lives, it is healthy to have relationships with others that vary from mere acquaintance to being intimate and loving.

What we need from another person may be many things, such as:

● a person with whom I can talk about work and be understood and who will not gossip to others

● a person who will accept me as I am

- a person who will be reliable in a crisis

- a person who will tell me honestly what they think

- a person who challenges me when I do not make sense

- a person who is stimulating and interesting

- a person who is fun to be with

- a person whom I can trust with my innermost thoughts and feelings

- a person who helps me to feel good about myself

It would be unrealistic to expect all of these things from one person. By getting to know as many people as possible, who will each fulfil some of these needs from time to time, we will build up a network of people who will be supportive in appropriate ways when we ask them. We will also need to give support to others in our network.

MANAGING TIME

Our use of time will be linked with the behavioural habits we have developed. Just as changing our behaviour will alter our susceptibility to stress, so will changing the way we use time be central to our stress fitness.

The first step is to clarify goals. What are we trying to do or achieve in the time available? Is it realistic and what we really want or need to do? This clarification can apply to any time-scale and to any life dimension – work, career, relationships, family, and so on. Previous chapters have focused on the importance of career and life-planning; time is another dimension in both of these activities and it is necessary to know what we want to achieve in it before we can use it effectively.

GOALS

Setting our own goals can be a daunting task. Often we think it is better not to set them at all in case we are disappointed! Maybe our goals have been submerged amongst other people's and perhaps we are not sure how valid it is for us to have goals anyway. On the other hand, we can be so caught up in the daily grind of striving to achieve targets that we are not sure what we want any more. We can feel pressurised at the very thought of further goal-setting!

Using the idea of long-, medium- and short-term goals is helpful. We can decide, for example, if long term is five years, medium term perhaps three years and short term one year; or long term might mean one year, medium term six months and short term one month. Even using this framework to plan for a week or a day can prove valuable, working back from the furthest goal and planning 'milestones' for achievements along the way. Doing this planning can have a powerful effect by focusing us on what we should be spending our time on as well as helping us to monitor progress, which can be very motivating. It is a procedure that can be used in any aspect of our lives.

Once the goals are set, it is easier to prioritise, plan for the future and organise our time.

PRIORITISING

Often we spend time doing all the *urgent* things and leave the *important* things to the end, when of course there is no time left for them. Or we try to do more than is possible, ending up feeling frustrated, annoyed that we have not achieved what we have set for ourselves and, as a consequence, overstressed. Similarly we can devote all our energies to responding to others' demands, being *reactive*, rather than focusing on our own goals and being *proactive*.

Prioritising involves putting those things to be done in order of *importance*. By prioritising we can also ensure that we are not just involved in routine *maintenance* tasks. We can decide to devote time to *progress* tasks that help us, our work, our department, our team and our organisation to move forward. For example, spending time on managing the stress levels in a team could lead to them being more productive in the long term.

TIME-WASTING

The last aspect of time management is to use what time we have effectively. Time-wasting can arise from habits that have become part of our behaviour but that we can choose to change. It can also result from the demands of others, which may be integral to our job of work and so more difficult to deal with. Either way they can stop us reaching our goals and be responsible for unhealthy stress.

The following time-wasters have been identified by people on Industrial Society courses:

THE TOP TWENTY-ONE TIME-WASTERS

1 Constant interruptions – telephone or other

2 Indecision

3 Meetings – too long or not really necessary

4 Switching priorities

5 Lack of objectives, priorities or daily plan

6 Personal disorganisation

7 Cluttered desk or work area

8 Ineffective delegation

9 Shuffling paper work

10 Limited access to required equipment or materials

11 Trying to find or track down people

12 Attempting too much – inability to say 'No'

13 'Butterflying' from job to job, leaving tasks unfinished

14 Inadequate, inaccurate, delayed information or communication

15 Unnecessary socialising

16 Office procedures not clearly established

17 Confused line of responsibility or authority, or the need to get decisions approved

18 Constant checking up on others and their work

19 Plunging into a task without planning

20 Lack of self-discipline

21 Exhaustion!

If we are clarifying our goals and prioritising, then time-wasting should be minimised. However we will have to confirm for ourselves any ways in which we do waste time and make sure they are not essential parts of our job.

WHAT YOU CAN DO ABOUT TIME-WASTERS

● Go through the list and identify those time-wasters you experience

● Check whether they are necessary. For example, if answering the telephone is part of your job it is not a time-waster

● For those left, see which ones you could do something about and work out what you need to do

● For any still left, consider how you could best cope to minimise the stress, for example letting go (see Chapter 5)

TRAINING FOR STRESS FITNESS

Stress fitness is one of the themes of this book and if we are to be fit then it will be necessary to train. The letters of the word TRAIN can be useful in helping us to remember the types of actions we can be taking to build up and maintain stress fitness.

T is for **talking**
R is for **relaxing**
A is for **activities**
I is for **interests**
N is for **nourishing**

The juggling act

Each area can be used as a means of support. By choosing activities relevant to us, while ensuring that we include some from each section, we can keep control over balancing our lives. (If you refer back to the questionnaire at the beginning of this chapter you will see that the statements were grouped in the same way.)

The lists that follow are by no means comprehensive. They are intended to generate further thinking. They may also help to pinpoint activities we already use and help us to recognise what we are doing already. (Stars against ideas indicate further information on this topic in the Resources section.)

Talking allows us to:

- face, explore and tackle problems

- express our feelings

- communicate our views and begin to manage particular pressures

- reflect and review

- enjoy the company of others

T FOR TALKING

While we are expressing our feelings we can be either getting negative feelings off our chest, sharing joy and delight or showing affection, compassion and love for others. Since human beings are social creatures, we all need the company of other people to varying degrees, be they acquaintances, colleagues, friends, family or intimate partners. Talking with people is one way of satisfying that need. Another way in which talking can help is by clarifying our thoughts, as long as the person we are talking to is a good listener! This is all part of building up our support networks too.

WHAT YOU CAN DO ABOUT TALKING

- Talk through something that is bothering you or creating pressure, with someone you trust

- Find time for reflection, which can include planning to discuss issues with another person

- Keep good communication channels open by talking about things at home or at work

- Join a club or class where there are likely to be people congenial to you

---

cont.

- Make time to meet people you like

- Join a political party and go to meetings

- Find out more about other people by showing an interest in what they think and feel and sharing some of your own thoughts and feelings with them

- If you have difficulty coming to terms with something in your life find a counsellor* or therapist

- Counselling* offers the total attention of a caring and non-judgemental person, someone to whom you can talk about any aspect of your life that may be troubling you or you feel could be improved. You will be helped and supported in finding your own solutions to problems

R FOR RELAXING

If we are leading stressful lives, whether we are enjoying that or not, we must make sure that there is time for relaxation. Because our response to high-pressure situations will include a bodily reaction, it is very important to learn to let go of tension. It is sometimes difficult to relax because we are often unaware that our muscles are tense until we suffer a headache or back pain, for example. With regular practice, however, we can learn to let go of the physical tensions associated with stress. We can even resist their build-up and reduce their impact.

It is possible to learn to relax and this involves developing body awareness – identifying the tension and learning to let it go.

Relaxation on the run There are quick exercises that can be done when the going is rough in a tense meeting, before a difficult interview, when someone has made a comment that we find hurtful or at any other time of pressure, without anyone else being aware of what we are doing. Practising these regularly will make them more effective for us.

Recharging Relaxing can be a way of 'recharging our batteries' and boosting our energy. To do this we need to make time for gentle activities like a quiet walk or reading a favourite magazine.

Fun activities are just as important in helping us to keep our balance. Laughter in particular can have physical, mental and emotional benefits and can often help us to put a sense of proportion back into our lives, as well as relaxing us.

It is very difficult to be stressed in a relaxed body!

WHAT YOU CAN DO ABOUT RELAXING AND RECHARGING

● **Relaxation on the run**

- Practise any of these quick relaxations frequently to stop the build-up of tensions

- Check through your body systematically and relax any muscles that are tensed

- Tense the muscles in your hands and feet and relax them again

- Relax your arms and shoulders

- Breathe more slowly and deeply

- Take two or three slow, deep breaths and then breathe easily again

- Let your body become still and relax your posture

- Relax your eyes by closing them or focusing on a distant point

- Instruct yourself to slow your movements, particularly if you are a dasher

- Five steps to stop the stress response:

  1 Smile to yourself

  2 Relax your jaw. Let your lips part slightly

  3 Very gently, breathe more slowly and deeply

  4 Say 'relax' to yourself at each out-breath

  5 Drop your shoulders and feel your spine lengthen

- To refocus, take 2 minutes to focus on your breathing. Let it deepen slightly. When thoughts enter your head, let them go. You can come back to them. After 2 minutes prioritise your activities

---

cont.

- Allow yourself to imagine clean pure water cleansing your body of all tensions or a warm sun melting away the tensions

● **Relaxing at leisure**

- Take up some form of *meditation**. There are different schools of meditation, of which transcendental meditation is perhaps the best known. Apart from refocusing the mind and relaxing the body, it is also claimed to enhance creative thinking

- There are many different kinds of *massage** with different aims – from repairing physical damage to encouraging balance between the physical, emotional and spiritual aspects of the human being. It is necessary to find the one that suits you

- *Reflexology** works on the theory that areas in the feet have connections with specific areas in the rest of the body. By gentle pressure and massage on the feet, imbalances caused by stress or injury can be redressed

- *Yoga** helps to balance the whole person – body, mind and spirit – by gentle exercises

- The *Alexander technique** gently relaxes the muscles and realigns the body so that it is more efficient

- *Hypnotherapy** helps by relaxing you and dealing with specific pressures and unhealthy stress

- *Aromatherapy** involves inhalation or massage with essential oils for mental and physical relaxation

- Make time for *recharging activities* – listening to music, taking a restful break, reading, walking – whatever gives you real pleasure

A FOR ACTIVITIES

To exercise the body   A survey from the Sports Council and the Health Education Authority published in 1992 found that at least seven out of ten men and eight out of ten women aged 16–74 did not undertake enough physical activity to keep them healthy. It is difficult to deal with life if we are not physically fit, and we need some exercise to keep our muscles toned and our metabolism working efficiently. There are a whole range of activities that we can choose from, to suit all ages and types of people.

Energetic exercise can help to burn off some of the energy that may have been generated by the pressures but has not had an outlet before. It can also go some way to releasing pent-up feelings.

If sleep has been disturbed by stress, another benefit of physical activity is that we usually feel relaxed afterwards and are able to sleep better.

To distract the mind   Spending energy doing something that involves us totally, both mentally and physically, can prove very powerful in the balancing act by taking our minds off the pressures.

Being assertive with stress   Developing assertive behaviour helps us to be more in control over what happens to us while being considerate to other people. It helps us to face difficulties and to take constructive action when pressure is high.

WHAT YOU CAN DO ABOUT ACTIVITIES

- Take regular (twice a week) physical exercise that you enjoy and that fits in with your routine and lifestyle

- Go for a walk

- Walk or cycle wherever you can instead of driving or taking a bus or train

- Swimming exercises most of the muscles without putting any strain on the back

- Dancing can also give pleasure from the music and company

- Sports* and jogging can be taken up at any level, but make sure that they are not adding extra pressure

- Join a gym

- Buy a rebounder (mini trampoline) or exercise bike

- Learn a new sport

---

cont.

- Gardening can be gentle or more active and can also provide opportunities for thinking things through; try some constructive destruction like pulling up convolvulus or digging the vegetable patch for getting rid of frustration or angry feelings!

- Get involved in local community activities

- Take up a creative and practical hobby (like sewing, painting, woodwork, cooking, pottery) that uses your mind and your body (remember that one person's pleasure is another person's pressure!)

- Enrol on an assertiveness* course

I FOR INTERESTS

Those of us who manage to retain a balance through periods of extreme pressure are often those who have an active interest that has no relationship with the stressful areas of our lives. These interests may be ones we pursue alone or with other people but they are ones that we have personally chosen. They may also be in areas that are completely separate from the rest of our lives and can help us to develop talents, skills and abilities that are not needed at work or at home. Interests can help us fulfil a number of our needs.

Emotions   Some interests, like music, literature, art and the other arts, can help us to keep in touch with our feelings and help us to express ourselves, whether we take part in them ourselves or appreciate them.

Beliefs   There are many ways of making sense of the world and our lives in it. It is helpful to work out our own values and what we consider to be of overall importance in our lives. In this way we are better prepared to deal with decisions or crises in a way that will give us a clearer idea of what we need to do.

Social   Participating in a shared interest can ensure that we spend time in social activities, which can give great satisfaction. This is also true of some of the activities in the previous section.

WHAT YOU CAN DO ABOUT INTERESTS

- Read books, magazines and papers that interest you

- Go to the theatre, the cinema and art galleries

- Take up a craft*, a hobby* or an interest* that occupies your mind and extends your skills or knowledge

- Do an Open University course*

- Do crossword puzzles

- Join a club or society whose subject sounds interesting

- Do something creative that takes up your whole attention like writing, making music or painting – as long as you can enjoy the activity without setting such high standards for yourself that you increase the pressure

- Choose things that interest you to watch on TV or to listen to on the radio

- Take up some form of voluntary work to contribute to the community and regain a sense of proportion

- If you want to explore your sense of purpose in life consider joining a religious group or reading philosophy

- Work out for yourself what is important to you by asking yourself these sorts of questions:

    - Who are the most important people in your life and who are the least? What is it about them that makes you feel this?

    - What are the values or ideas about life that you would not be prepared to compromise?

    - What events in your life have had a big effect on you? Why do you think that is so?

    - What activities give you most satisfaction? What is it about them that is satisfying?

    - If you were shipwrecked on a desert island who and what would you miss most?

N FOR NOURISHING

Physically   There are many ways of nourishing ourselves but unless we are properly nourished physically we can often not think straight and our feelings may be muddled. Countless diets make all sorts of claims and in some cases they will work. The essential thing is to find one that is balanced and that suits us individually. It may be necessary to experiment because we have different needs at different ages or when we are engaged in different activities; if we enjoy energetic sports we will need different nutrients from someone who takes up knitting.

Equally important is the consideration of what not to take into our bodies. Plenty of information is available about nicotine, alcohol, caffeine and drugs and the harm they can do. They may have a temporary effect that feels beneficial but are likely to cause serious damage to health and well-being if abused.

A number of therapies can be particularly nourishing as they help us maintain a physical and emotional balance as well as maintaining good health.

Emotionally   Some people get emotional, mental and spiritual nourishment from their talking, relaxing, activities and interests, but having treats is important too. Even if we are not given them by other people we can give ourselves pleasure regularly by allowing ourselves to do something that we do not usually do and that makes us feel really spoiled. The treat does not need to cost money; it can be something quite simple that pleases us. If we can afford it, it can be an occasional luxury.

WHAT YOU CAN DO ABOUT NOURISHING
● Find a diet that has a good balance to suit your physique and lifestyle
● Make sure that you eat plenty of fresh fruit, vegetables and salad
● Keep to the limits of alcohol consumption set out by the Health Education Authority* – about 21 units for men and 14 units for women spread over a week; but remember we all react differently to alcohol at different times

- Take fewer than three drinks of coffee, tea, chocolate or cola a day

- If you feel that you are, or are in danger of becoming, dependent on alcohol*, drugs* or any other substance, contact an appropriate agency

- Cook a special meal or go out to one; the odd indulgence, even though not in line with a healthy diet, does no harm

- Remember that these general guidelines are fine unless you have special dietary needs, when you need the advice of a doctor or dietician

- Keep your weight to the right level for your age, height and build

- If being under pressure makes you sweat more, make sure you drink extra water

- After a particularly stressful or energetic time, have a hot bath with your favourite bath oil

- Make sure that at least once a day you do something solely for your pleasure

- Acupuncture* restores balance in the body's energies with needles that prick only a little or not at all

- Chiropractic* relieves any strain or distortion that may have happened through being stressed, and restores a balanced flow of energy through the body

- Kinesiology* uses massage to restore energy imbalance and maintain good health and well-being

- Homoeopathy* is a form of medicine that works on the principle that the body should be encouraged to heal itself. It is also concerned with maintaining good health

- Osteopathy* repairs skeletal and muscular damage or distortion (which can be caused by stress) by manipulation and massage

- Shiatsu* is a gentle form of pressure and massage that connects with the acupuncture points and restores the body's energy balance

cont.

- Give yourself treats. A treat does not need to be something expensive, particularly if one of the worries you have is about money. A treat is something that makes you feel really great

MEMO

Remember that we all need to be doing something in each area of T R A I N to build and maintain stress fitness.

PART III

MANAGING STRESS

Managing Through Stress 8

One definition of a manager is someone who achieves results through others. Part of the job is to make sure that work is done as quickly and as efficiently as possible. Whilst this inevitably involves making demands on staff, the way we do this will result in them feeling either healthily challenged by the tasks or suffering unhealthy stress. Managers often feel that, because they would be able to cope and respond positively to the demands they are making, everyone else should be able to do the same. While members of staff must be able to fulfil their roles up to an agreed standard, there may be times when this is difficult, either because of pressures outside work, or because the demands are unrealistic.

Because someone is generally able to cope with a particular workload does not necessarily mean that they can always perform at that pace without periods of recovery. Conversely, when they are in the Peaks, new demands seem less daunting because they are feeling positive about meeting the latest challenge. Each situation needs to be seen afresh as far as stress is concerned. The stress manager's aim is to keep each person performing at his or her peak keeping them healthily stressed to do this. This will also entail dealing with the unhealthy aspects – helping people off the overstress Spiral or moving them up the understress Steps.

Example: Jean

Jean is an able member of your staff whom you would like to develop with a view to promotion. You know she is keen to progress and is willing to take on extra work to that end. However, you do not know a great deal about her personally and may unwittingly find yourself sending her into the overstress Spiral, rather than utilising the creative energy of healthy stress.

In the appraisal interview you identify areas she is keen to develop and arrange appropriate training. In addition, to extend her experience you give her a new project, which entails several trips abroad. The challenge of these extra tasks may well generate extra energy for Jean, raising her performance and taking her into the Peaks. However, she could begin to sink into the Spiral if the additional pressures are not taken into account. For example, she has a trainee in her department requiring development time, she is nervous about her presentation skills and she is spending extra personal time brushing up her languages for the new project.

If she is stress fit she may well be able to manage these demands and constraints and continue at peak performance for a while. However, changes outside work – of which you may be unaware – could create extra pressure and reduce her capacity. For example, family financial worries and a sick child could tip the balance, unless she is able to increase her supports. As her manager you have the potential to help her do this.

You may well feel that Jean's life outside work is no concern of yours. However, it will be harder to stop the momentum of her sliding down the Spiral than to take action to prevent it.

We have seen in Part I and Chapter 4 some of the signs of unhealthy stress. The most significant ones for the manager relate to the work output and business goals: contracts lost, customer complaints, deadlines and targets not met, conflict in the team, higher absenteeism than usual and lower standards than required. Not only can these be indications that the individuals concerned are over- or understressed but they can also generate the stress virus and infect other people – including the manager – or signal the presence of the stress vacuum with its demoralising effects.

What can we do to make people perform at their best and meet the challenge of stressful situations constructively? How can we optimise the stress response, to ensure that it is healthy stress we generate and not the unhealthy overstress or understress? What people give back to the organisation will reflect the ways in which they are valued and this can be communicated through the management style. The stress manager puts stress at the centre of the management process.

WHAT YOU CAN DO TO BECOME A STRESS MANAGER

- Consider whether you impose your own need for stress on others and whether you pass on the stress virus

- Know your staff well as individuals

- Recognise the culmulative pressures on them

- Be aware of their lives outside work (this does not mean knowing everything about them)

- Recognise that it is better to spend some time being understanding and encouraging than to have people off sick

- Aim to generate challenge appropriate for each person's need for stress to keep them in the Peaks

- Read on ...

MANAGEMENT STYLE – PRESSURE OR SUPPORT?

The manager's management style is an important factor in employees' experience of stress in the workplace. Management practices and procedures have the potential to generate or eradicate the pressures, to build or demolish stress fitness.

American research by Robert Golembiewski (1986) found that the clearest indicator of burn-out was how the employee was treated by his or her direct supervisor. When people were treated with respect, care and compassion they responded with more commitment and productivity. More recently, Herriot, Gibbons and Pemberton (1992), of Sundridge Park Management Centre, found that managers themselves rate 'being treated fairly' higher than they rate salary or status in relation to job satisfaction. This suggests that feeling unfairly treated would create dissatisfaction and greater pressure.

How do we deal with our staff when they are suffering unhealthy stress? Common reactions are to continue in exactly the same way or even to impose greater demands – after all, we still have deadlines to reach. Our team's stress can become just another pressure for us to handle, and it is interesting that we often react to other people's stress in the same way that we react to our own. However, managing through stress requires a recognition that each team member will respond in a unique way.

Of course, pressure can often produce a healthy response. But if the staff members concerned are not stress fit and perceive an uncomfortable imbalance between the demands, constraints and supports both in and out of work, then they will feel less able to cope with the pressures we impose.

As managers we will not usually be aware of what is going on for people outside work, and if there are a number of life changes creating pressure this can affect work performance. It is sometimes possible for people to leave worries about home behind when they go to work, but it is unlikely that this can be sustained for long periods of time. Feelings influence perception and when people are on the downward Spiral, feeling stretched and harassed – perhaps by situations outside work – it is easy for them to exaggerate the size of new work demands and see these as threatening.

PICKING UP ON STRESS

We have already considered in Chapter 1 how difficult it is to admit to stress in the workplace, and the damage that can be done if we do not bring it into the open. The stress manager needs to ensure that the relationship is such that staff members can talk about difficulties in coping and what is bothering them. Clearly it is not appropriate or desirable that the manager should expect to understand or know everything that is going on for people all of the time. However, if the manager takes time to work at being both approachable and observant, this will make it easier to pick up on potential stress problems before they get out of hand and harm work output.

Approachability will develop if employees feel that the manager takes a personal interest in them and is prepared to allow time for the talking that builds a relationship. This does not mean endless chatting about leisure activities or family life, but it does mean genuine interest in how people are getting on and communication of an attitude of individual respect. The beliefs discussed in Chapter 5 are relevant here. Positive relationships can make the difference between staff feeling cooperative and motivated or unwilling and reluctant.

Each manager will choose to develop relationships in his or her own way, yet trust is a part of approachability. This can be developed by consistency of behaviour, taking time to show care and concern for people in the workplace and reliability of action. Clearly the manager must manage his or her own stress to be able to deal constructively with that in team members; it will not be helpful if disclosure of feeling overloaded is met with irritation or anger from the manager!

As we have seen in Chapter 4, there are definite characteristics which can point to understress, overstress or healthy stress. A change in someone's behaviour will only be recognisable if the manager is aware of usual patterns of behaviour, gathered through regular, unobtrusive observation and two-way communication. Once noticed, the manager needs to take action and do something about it.

Example: Georgina

Georgina had noticed that one of her staff, Philip, appeared less cheerful than usual and that his performance had deteriorated. She was extremely busy herself and did not feel she could spare much time to find out what was happening to him.

She contrived to sit with him at lunch in the canteen one day and asked how things were going. He seemed reluctant to expand on his reply that he was fine, yet with gentle questioning and her concerned observation that he appeared to be less happy with the job, he told her how difficult he was finding a particular task that she had delegated. He was bothered about not reaching his targets and couldn't work out why the job was not progressing smoothly.

Her enquiries revealed that he had not received adequate instruction on the computer program he was using. By arranging this, the job was done. Spending time with Philip meant she picked up the problem and avoided further ones.

WHAT YOU CAN DO TO PICK UP ON STRESS

● Consider if you make yourself available and approachable so that people can talk if they choose

● Develop approachability by:

– Getting to know people and how they are
– Listening to their views on an informal basis
– Generally showing an interest in people and what they are doing without getting caught up in too much unnecessary detail
– Devoting time to this aspect of managing
– Giving full attention to staff when you are with them
– Looking out for early warning signs of inability to cope and taking action. Read on for this ...

COMMUNICATION

Sharing information, letting people know what is happening and what is expected of them, listening, and responding to what they say are important tools in the management of stress. Lack of communication, either at work or in more personal matters, will act as a constraint. Most of us have experienced situations where even a small piece of information would have helped or even prevented unhealthy stress building up to an uncomfortable level. For example, if it has not been made clear who is in charge of a particular project, or if we do not know that our work is below standard, this can give rise to unnecessary disputes or leave others affected by inefficiency and the individual concerned upset by the atmosphere.

Some specific communication techniques will help to ensure that it is stress that is managed in the team and not overstress that is being mopped up. If, as managers, we do not know what our staff are doing and thinking or about any difficulties people are experiencing, then we may well be making inadequately informed decisions.

Similarly, if people are not told about what is happening in the organisation, there is almost certain to be a rumour process at work based on half-heard or half-understood information. If people know, even in broad terms, what is happening and what is likely to happen, the mis-information that is circulated will lose its potential for anxiety, disruption and consequent unhealthy stress. There is also a greater likelihood of cooperative problem-solving and future planning.

Exchange of information links closely with the issue of control. The tightly controlling approach is often sustained by a fear that things will not be done as well or as quickly if choice is allowed. However, a very low level of control or choice can create a workplace experience of insecurity and frustration, which is unlikely to encourge peak performance at the best of times, and is likely to put us into the downward Spiral at those extra-busy moments.

Control over what we do at work is an important feature in job satisfaction, as is using one's knowledge and experience to make decisions – these were ranked as important aspects of work in the Henley Centre's 1988 survey. Similarly, the B*lueprint* survey (Webb, 1989) found that employees who can help solve problems are twice as likely to rate the company as well managed and are more committed to helping it to be successful.

A sharing of wisdom and experience – not a monopoly of management – makes the organisation more effective in the long run. We can reduce overstress and generate more commitment by giving as much control and choice as is possible to the workforce – one American company goes as far as inviting people to choose their own job titles.

If we can trust people to deliver (having ensured of course that they are clear about what they are expected to deliver and have the skills required) and monitor carefully and appropriately to pick up on performance, not only will we be generating the conditions for maximum performance but we will be helping to build up stress fitness.

WHAT YOU CAN DO TO INCREASE CERTAINTY AND CONTROL

- Ensure that lines of communication are clear and well used

- Foster a climate of frank exchange where people's opinions receive a fair hearing

- Find out people's views on their work organisation and consult them on decisions that affect them

- Tell people of developments that are likely to affect them, in good time

---

cont.

- Encourage those who work together to share information about what they are doing and why

- Allow people where possible to decide how to manage their own work loads

- Listen carefully to what people have to say and let them influence what happens as much as possible

- Look for opportunities to devolve greater control to team members

- Examine opportunities for involvement in decision-making and procedural changes for both teams and individuals

- Discuss career progress and training opportunities with your people

CHANGE

It is significant that even changes that are welcomed still stress us and making adjustments can use up a great deal of time and energy. Because the introduction of changes and the management of the process will affect the long-term morale of those involved, a great deal of care is necessary.

Many models have been developed of the stages associated with reactions to both life and work changes. In essence people will typically move forwards, and perhaps backwards, through:

1 shock
2 avoidance/resistance
3 acceptance
4 adaptation and integration

The ease with which people progress through the stages will reflect the following factors:

- whether they have been involved in initiating the change

- whether they welcome or fear it

- how well in advance they have been informed about it

- how much control they have over it

- how much they know about it

- whether they have any influence on how it is implemented

- how clear they are about how or why it is to be implemented

Because we can be so keen to push a change through quickly, a common mistake is to try to avoid the process. It may seem uncomfortable for the manager, yet by recognising and acknowledging the unhealthy stress others may be experiencing, we can take actions appropriate at each stage to smooth the transition. By ignoring – and not actively managing – the process, we will prolong it.

Any announcement of imminent change needs careful handling to ensure that leaks do not give rise to rumours and scare-mongering. At the same time, early announcement of change leaves time for proper consultation and modification of the plan. The best time to press ahead with the implementation of change is after real discussion and consultation have been possible. The change process is more likely to proceed smoothly if time has been devoted to gaining the backing of the people who will make it work, recognising that some will need more time to readjust.

WHAT YOU CAN DO TO INTRODUCE CHANGE WITH LEAST UNHEALTHY STRESS

At the shock stage:

- Give as much information as possible about the reasons for the change and what its effects are likely to be for both the staff and the organisation

- Be clear about the timing and processes that will take place

- Cover both the beneficial aspects and the less welcome aspects

- Allow some discussion of both, accepting the expression of the negative feelings and thoughts people may have initially, but also encouraging exploration of the possible benefits

- Allow time for things to sink in

- Be available for support during the whole process

cont.

At the avoidance/resistance stage:

- Assure people that the change will happen

- Listen to and acknowledge people's feelings

- Respond to the concerns that people raise

- Invite further suggestions and allow people affected to influence how the change will be implemented

- Accept that tension or discomfort is an essential part of the process

At the acceptance stage:

- Be prepared to utilise fully the extra energy released here

- Set goals and priorities and monitor movement towards them

- Help people to manage necessary adjustments to working practices as far as possible themselves

- Look out for other procedures that might need to change as a result

- Continue to support

At the adaptation and integration stage:

- Pay tribute to contributions people have made in helping the change take place while it is happening and when the change has been made

- Recognise the achievement in implementing the change

- Be alert to signs that indicate that the change may not be fully integrated and take appropriate action

- Let people get on with it

STEPS TO MANAGING STRESS

BRIEFING AND DELEGATION

A great deal of confusion and overstress can be generated by failure to brief and delegate adequately. For people to have security they need to know what is expected of them, whether the task is intrinsic to their job or is a newer task that is being delegated. Clear and full communication is vital.

A clear job specification and a good induction and training programme help enormously. In addition, the boundaries of how much, by when and to what standard should be made explicit. The lines of accountability should be clear, as should details of what support is available and where essential information can be obtained, as well as the ways in which performance will be monitored.

WHAT YOU CAN DO TO MAKE BRIEFING EFFECTIVE

- Ensure that your induction of staff is clear and thorough

- Ensure that people understand what tasks are expected of them and to what standard

- Tell them how their efforts contribute to the targets of the department and the aims of the organisation

- Let people know how they are doing. Reinforce success to create a feeling of achievement. Give constructive criticism where appropriate

---

WHAT YOU CAN DO TO MAKE DELEGATING EFFECTIVE

- Decide what can be delegated

- Choose the most suitable person

- Find out if they are willing and able

- Be specific about what you are delegating and the limits

- Provide training or coaching if needed

- Agree what authority they might need and arrange it

- Set standards for quality

- Provide resources, including access to you if needed

- Monitor progress at agreed times and let the person know what they are doing well and what they might improve

- Give recognition for tasks achieved

- Recognise that you are still accountable

LISTENING

It is just as important to have skills for effectively receiving information from our staff as it is to communicate relevant information to them clearly. If we are not well informed, about either things that are happening in the workplace or other people's thoughts and feelings, then our decisions may well turn out to be useless because we are not aware of all the factors that need to be taken into consideration. Too often lip-service is paid to listening and consulting when it is clear that the manager has no intention of taking any notice of what has been said: this is likely to set up very unhealthy forms of stress and lead to alienation.

Active listening is an important skill for managers, and one of the main ways we demonstrate our care for staff. It involves showing not only that we have heard what we have been listening to, but also that we are prepared to take account of what we have heard.

It is often difficult to do for many reasons. We may feel that:

● there is no time

● we know best because we have more information

● we do not respect the other people's judgement

● we are in too much turmoil ourselves to be able to give the other person any attention

● we do not want to risk hearing something that will lead to more worries for us.

There are ways of demonstrating that we have listened properly. We can show through our body language and facial expression that the speaker has our full attention. We can reflect back in our own words what we think we have heard to check out if we have heard accurately and understood. We can make sure that our questions pick up on what has been said and are not on an unconnected subject.

WHAT YOU CAN DO TO SHOW THAT YOU ARE LISTENING ACTIVELY
● Look at the person without staring
● Nod or 'mm' when a point has been made

- Ask open questions to get accurate information. These usually begin with the words 'what', 'how', 'when', 'where', or 'who'

- Check if you have understood by tentatively repeating what the person has said but in different words

- Avoid being immediately critical of what is being said. If you have to disagree make sure that this is said considerately and after you have tried to understand what the other person means

CONSULTING

Listening is the basis of any consultation process and through this people can feel that they are contributing to management and can also find out what is going on. Again, the key factor in consultation is to make sure that it is not just an empty exercise, which could create unhealthy stress.

The manager still has responsibility for decisions and is accountable for any consequences. However, there may well be a wealth of ideas and constructive suggestions available from staff, which can mean that decisions will be more likely to lead to success. So that staff understand that they have been taken seriously when they have been consulted, there must be some follow-up to outline how they have influenced decisions or why their suggestions were not taken up. In this way the next time they are consulted they will, perhaps, be in a position to make even better suggestions.

MONITORING

Monitoring performance is essential for the maintenance of standards and to ensure the manager really knows what is going on. The manager can also use the monitoring process to detect the early signs of unhealthy stress.

It is generally known that good managers spend about 60 per cent of their time face to face with other people. One of the best ways of keeping in contact with what is really going on and of making people feel valued is frequently to walk round the workplace, talking and listening to people. This gives opportunities to chat informally about work issues, check progress on specific tasks or initiatives, and develop positive and open relationships. It will also encourage the kind of relationship in which discussion about unhealthy stress is possible.

GIVING AND RECEIVING FEEDBACK

It is essential for anyone with a management responsibility to give detailed feedback on work performance. Many people in work are unaware of how they are getting on: whether their work is up to the expected standard, how it compares with others', if they are doing it in the most effective way, what they are doing really well and what they might need to improve. This can lead to uncertainty, anxiety and unhealthy stress. Most people need, at least sometimes, to see that their achievements have been recognised and also to know what more might be expected of them.

Annual reporting systems and appraisal interviews can be more or less helpful depending on the attitude and skill of the interviewer and also the attitude of the interviewee. It is not enough, however, to rely on the once-yearly meeting, as too much can be happening during the year that may need attention. Good feedback involves offering information regarding the performance of specific tasks and reactions to that performance.

All too often, however, a feeling of not wanting to upset the other person and not knowing how to encourage them to recognise what has gone wrong or how to put it right gets in the way of giving criticism. There are also inhibitions about giving people praise because they might demand more pay or become too complacent. It must be realised though that unless people know what they are good at and what they need to improve, and this is communicated in a helpful way, they will not be able or willing to do anything about it.

Informing colleagues about the effects of their work or behaviour on us can be a useful way of improving communication. In addition, if we want to act in future from an informed basis, and learn from past experiences, then we too need to be open to receiving feedback.

WHAT YOU CAN DO TO GIVE FEEDBACK EFFECTIVELY

- Be specific about what the person has done, with examples

- If there is a need to be critical be sure to give some positive point first so that the person can be encouraged to build on success. Both positive and negative feedback are needed for someone to be willing to make the effort to improve

---

- Offer your comments in a manner that shows clearly that you are trying to be helpful

- Make sure that you are commenting on what the person says and does, not on their personality

- Make it clear when you are giving your opinion as opposed to reporting facts

- Listen carefully to what the person thinks and feels about what you have said

- Also check that they have understood what you mean, that they accept it and that they have the ability to act on it

---

WHAT YOU CAN DO TO RECEIVE FEEDBACK AND USE IT CONSTRUCTIVELY

- Listen carefully

- Ask for clarification if you do not understand

- Ask for specific information and examples if they are not forthcoming

- Try not to feel defensive

- After clarifying what is meant, be prepared to challenge (with facts) criticism you feel is inaccurate

- Make clear that you are accepting criticism if you feel it is valid

- Be willing to change what you do if the feedback is useful

- If the feedback is positive, accept it and thank the giver!

CONFRONTING PROBLEMS

In the manager's role, it is essential to confront problems that relate to the work. Allowing problems or conflicts to build up can lead to unnecessary tension, both for ourselves and for our team and colleagues, with possibly disastrous consequences for the organisation. By facing the situation in a constructive and proactive way we can stop the unhealthy stress building up, and can take action to manage the situation.

We shall be looking at ways of dealing with conflict – one of the issues that we might prefer to avoid – in Chapter 9. Other examples of difficult issues are: the giving of bad news, the tackling of the really difficult task, intervening in a work group with a new approach, facing a colleague we find difficult or confronting a major personal change such as a new job or move. The list is endless, each person having his or her own avoidance areas.

One way of approaching really difficult situations is to identify the risks and rewards we assume the situation holds. We will often treat unknown or strange situations as threatening because we feel that the risks outweigh the rewards. Such situations are likely to cause unhealthy stress, especially if we lack confidence about our abilities in such situations. Having opportunities for reflection and review, with friends and trusted colleagues, can help us translate the experience of the new situation into guidelines for the future.

Example: Keith

Keith could see that his team were not working together as effectively as they might and that he needed to discuss this with them and agree some changes. He felt reluctant to do this though, and kept putting it off. Talking it through with a colleague, he identified that his reluctance stemmed from a previous experience when, as a member of a team, a similar team review had left individuals feeling angry that their views had not been taken into account, with the effect that performance had actually diminished. He realised that as the manager he could ensure that this did not happen and felt more confident to approach the situation.

We may have internal pressures which work against us. We may have been encouraged as children not to take risks because we are bound to fail. We may have learnt that we should only ever take on something new if we have evidence that we can do it, or not to expect much of ourselves. We might have been encouraged to see ourselves as slower or less able in comparison with our peers, or as having skills only in particular areas. We may have been taught not to dwell on or talk about feelings or never to upset people. All these can discourage us from approaching new situations. On the other hand, a tendency to strive for new challenges can also create unhealthy stress because we overload ourselves and do not adjust to the demands of the current situation.

WHAT YOU CAN DO TO HELP CONFRONT DIFFICULT SITUATIONS

When faced with a problem situation, such as a new challenge or difficult task, consider and list:

- All the potential *risks* you identify in the situation

- All the potential *rewards* you identify in the situation

Now decide:

- Are you overestimating or underestimating the risks and rewards?

- Is your tendency to focus more on risks or more on rewards?

- How might this awareness affect the way you approach a problem situation?

- What supports do you need to minimise the risks?

- How might you use the rewards to support you?

- Do you need to develop any further skills to help in the situation, such as assertiveness or feedback skills? If so, plan how you will do this and use this book

---

Building up our supports is an important tool in helping us confront difficult situations. In the absence of accurate information we may well feel unhealthily stressed, so clarifying the facts can help. Similarly, an undefined problem can seem much larger and thus more daunting than it actually is. Focusing on the extent of the problem, and then breaking it into manageable chunks, each one to be tackled step by step, will help reduce the pressure.

WHAT YOU CAN DO TO SOLVE PROBLEMS

- Identify the problem in specific terms

- Collect relevant information

- Plan how you can approach it. If necessary, break it into manageable chunks

- Explore all possible solutions

- Choose the one that seems most appropriate

- List the actions that will need to be taken

- Make sure that these happen

- Review the process and, if necessary, repeat it

STRESS COACHING

So what do we do if we uncover a stress problem in the team? How can we tackle it constructively? The following framework for a stress interview can be used to enable us to coach someone who is suffering unhealthy stress that is adversely affecting – or could affect – their work. These are essentially counselling skills.

It is important to remember that the manager is not attempting to solve the problem but, through listening, is allowing the person to focus on it and explore options to help them through a particularly tough patch. Sometimes it will be appropriate to provide extra support or resources; if necessary a referral to a counselling service can help (see Chapter 10). The aim is to explore alternative actions for the particular situation and also, in the long term, to develop stress fitness.

WHAT YOU CAN DO TO STRESS COACH

- Set up an informal interview in a quiet place where you will not be disturbed

- Comment on your observations and invite the person to talk about their concerns

- Emphasise that you are willing to help

- Use active listening skills as outlined earlier in this chapter and show interest and concern in the person's well-being

---

- Use open questions to encourage exploration of the problem

- Get the person to focus on what is causing the pressures and decide what they would like to happen, or the help that is needed, and where this might be available

- Consider offering a temporary reduction of work pressure, if appropriate, or other supports in your power, but make clear any definite expectations you have regarding future performance

- If the problem appears overwhelming, encourage the person to seek professional help or refer to an internal welfare department

- Agree a plan of action and follow up if possible

THE PROBLEM OF UNDERSTRESS

The *Blueprint* survey (Webb, 1989) found that 50 per cent of unskilled manual workers said that they could do more work in their current job without too much effort. In addition it identified that one effect of workforce reductions in the 1980s, new technology and increasing flexibility in the workplace has been to depress the skills and reduce the job interest of the lowest-grade workers. Overall, one-third of all respondents felt under-used at work. The potential for understress here is significant.

It is clear that certain repetitive jobs give little scope for involvement. Having a variety of things to do was identified as the third most important aspect of work in the Henley Centre's survey of 1988. Work design techniques can address this problem and encourage progress up the Steps. The following techniques to increase variety and satisfaction can be useful:

- job rotation – moving from task to task

- job enlargement – adding more tasks of a similar level

- job enrichment – adding more scope to a job to make better use of autonomous work groups, with the team being given greater participation in how the work is carried out, either with or without a leader.

When considering job design at any level of any organisation, the following checklist, developed by the TUC (1988), identifies ways to make effective use of employees' potential for responding positively to pressure.

JOB DESIGN CHECKLIST

Well-designed jobs should:

- provide opportunity for learning

- lead to some future desired by the job holders

- enable people to contribute to decisions affecting their jobs and the goals of the organisations

- have clear goals and expectations

- provide a degree of challenge

- provide adequate training and information

Tasks should:

- combine to form a coherent job, either alone or with related jobs

- provide a variety of pace, method and location

- demand a variety of skills

- have channels for the provision of feedback

- provide a degree of discretion in carrying out successive tasks

- carry responsibility for outcomes

- allow some control of work

Tasks should not:

- require completion in a time determined not by the workers but by the machine or system

- be short cycle

- create social deprivation

RESULTS AND COMMITMENT

It must be clear by now that managing stress constructively involves all the management practices and skills that are nowadays considered to be effective. If we find it possible to manage in the ways outlined in the 'What You Can Do' lists, we are likely to end up with staff that have a great deal of commitment to their work, to us their managers and to the organisation as a whole.

Respecting our staff and giving them as much control over their work and its environment as is reasonable will relieve the effects of both the demands we may make on them and any constraints. Supporting staff well will pay dividends in terms of attendance, morale and efficiency, as well as contributing to good relationships with suppliers, customers and other bodies important to our work. It will also help us to cope with the rate of change that is an inevitable part of workplaces today. In this way we shall be creating an atmosphere of cooperation in which there will be healthy stress levels without too much unhealthy stress.

9 Stress in Teams

INDIVIDUALS IN TEAMS

TEAM STRESS

Most people work with or alongside others to some extent. In effect, they are part of a team. For many of us, the people we work with will significantly influence our experience of our job; some teams work powerfully and productively together, and some seem fraught with pressures and tensions.

Our team membership will affect our stress fitness. It can either depressurise a difficult situation or be a source of pressure – constantly or at a particular moment in time. Team membership can act as a support, helping us to meet our demands, or it can serve as a constraint, making it more difficult for us to meet them.

Example: Jasmine

Jasmine had been looking forward to her new job in a smaller organisation. After a month she was thinking the move had been a mistake.

She felt under great pressure not only from the considerable challenges of the job but also from her team membership. There was little attempt at the cooperative working essential to the job, meetings were infrequent and information she needed for her work was not readily shared. In her previous job an established and close-knit team had solved problems together, provided mutual support and produced excellent results. The enjoyment of this was in stark contrast to the backbiting, unhelpfulness and poor results of the new team. Unless action was taken, Jasmine's stress fitness would be depleted in the new team.

We have all experienced periods of pressure at work. For each one our need is different at that particular moment. Perhaps we need to be left alone and given a wide berth; perhaps a sympathetic listening ear or someone to nudge us to prioritise our demands is called for; maybe practical assistance or confidence-building are the order of the day; or we need reassurance that our colleagues will not be offended by our temporary grumpiness or short temper. The way our colleagues relate to us will certainly influence our handling of the situation, assisting us in getting through a tough patch or making it more difficult.

TEAM STRESS RESPONSE

Teams, just like the individuals they comprise, develop habits of dealing with stress.

If an overstressed individual avoids the problem, by absenteeism or longer lunch breaks, a colleague may react in the same way, with increased problems of non-performance mounting up, or by picking arguments or disagreements. The first individual's response generates pressure for her or his colleague, whose response will affect other team members. The result is an entire team in unhealthy stress.

Often patterns of reactions develop in teams, with, for example the whole team 'frozen' by the pressures and unable to take action: an acute case of the stress virus! Clearly there are implications for work performance here, resulting in further unhealthy stress for the team leader, manager or the team itself.

THE IMPORTANCE OF TEAMS

An organisation's success depends on more than the performance of individuals. It also depends on the quality of the interaction between individuals – the extent to which they work together within a team and communicate effectively across teams.

A team can be viewed as a group of people who just happen to work together, either because of what they do or the organisational structure, for the purposes of management and monitoring, or because of interconnected targets. Or a team can be viewed as a source of creative energy, where relationships produce more than the sum of the parts: a synergistic team. Successful organisations are aware of the impact of attention to team basics. They will know how to make teams work to harness energy and commitment, minimising the destructive effects of unhealthy stress and generating the dynamic of healthy stress. Successful companies find ways of encouraging difference, recognising that therein lies the potential for employee involvement, creative solutions and powerful problem-solving.

The Blueprint survey (Webb, 1989) found that teamwork is widespread in organisations. Those who work for companies where teamwork and interdepartmental cooperation are high rate the company and its management higher and express greater job satisfaction, involvement and commitment to the company's success.

Teams, however, do not just happen. They need work and persistence if they are to generate greater organisational success and create stress fitness. The 'Hows' of the team are significant:

● how it is put together (and disbanded)

● how people are inducted into and leave it

● how it organises its work as a whole

● how an individual's work connects with and is dependent on others

● how it communicates, reviews, evaluates performance

● how people feel about their team membership

Each member of the organisation may well work in a number of different types of teams; for example:

● the permanent work-based or functional team – e.g. administration or sales team

● the coordinating or linking team – e.g. marketing, personnel

● the cross-functional team or horizontal team of peers – e.g. departmental heads, senior policy group or project managers

● the limited-life project team, e.g. working party or task force

In short-term project teams the limited time-scales can mean that procedures do not get fixed and unhealthy stress is limited. In addition, the challenge of the project goal can generate healthy stress. However, the shorter the time-scale the more important the procedures. Teams that fluctuate in composition and have flexible targets have a very great need to clarify their objectives and working procedures if they are going to respond and adapt effectively to change.

PROJECT TEAMS

Whilst we have considered individual signs of unhealthy stress in Chapter 4, the following features will indicate understress or overstress in the team. There will obviously be serious consequences, whatever the nature of the business:

HOW TO RECOGNISE UNHEALTHY STRESS IN THE TEAM

- tasks not achieved

- language focuses on 'I' not 'we'

- sickness, absence, unpunctuality

- covering up mistakes

- cold or hostile atmosphere

- little trust or reliability

- deadlines not met

- talking not related to work

- backbiting, gossip, alliances, in and out groups

- some members not contributing or making a poor contribution

- sulking

- little communication

- work below acceptable or possible standards

- little acknowledgement of each other

- lack of cooperation

- power struggles

- put-downs

- high staff turnover

- long lunch breaks

By contrast, a **healthily stressed team**:

- creates and makes the most of challenge

- balances the pressures within the team and finds ways to build support

- monitors its achievements and learns from the successes plus any other outcomes, turning negatives into learning points

- generally works together harmoniously, building on the individual contributions, using conflicting views and achieving synergy

- achieves the tasks set to the highest quality of achievement possible, whilst developing skills to enhance future performance

- makes full use of the available resources, with each member contributing to his or her highest potential

TEAM BASICS

These features provide the underpinnings for an effective and appropriately stressed team.

CLEAR GOALS

First and foremost teams have work to do. Individuals need to deliver a certain performance collectively to meet the team goals, and will often be evaluated on the basis of team achievements.

Lack of clarity or understanding of what the team is aiming to achieve is a major source of unhealthy stress. Each team member needs to be very clear about his or her goals, how they relate to the team goals and how these team goals relate to the organisation's goals. A clear and shared vision can act as a powerful focus for direction and endeavour.

WHAT YOU CAN DO TO CLARIFY TEAM GOALS

With your team:

● Answer the question: What is this team trying to achieve?

● Draft a clear outline of the purpose of the team: a mission statement

● Consider each person's part in the purpose and agree · in the team where each job fits in

---

It is important that the team contains people with the skills and experience necessary to do the job. Unhealthy stress is often a result of under- or overstaffing, overlap or duplication of skills, or skill deficiency. Team members can have too much or too little to do, too much or too little responsibility and involvement. They may need to check unnecessarily with others before progressing with their work, or take much longer than the job needs because they have not been adequately briefed or trained.

TEAM COMPOSITION

Example: George's team

George worked in a small team that organised international conferences. Increasingly, when events were imminent, the team members put in extremely long hours tying up loose ends and correcting errors that had slipped through. The stress virus generated in the team meant deadlines were nearly missed and a contract was in jeopardy.

When they took time to review their working procedures and the team composition it became apparent that they had an overlap of job roles and a major skills gap. Individuals were using their creative strengths in different directions with no one taking a clear coordinating role. Reorganisation enabled them to eradicate unhealthy stress and be much more effective.

For some individuals in the team, too little variety will lead to boredom and frustration, which may find an outlet in unconstructive activity. For others, too many demands will lead to overstress, which can, in the long term, reduce effectiveness and harm working relationships. Assessing the skills, experience and job demands of each team member against a checklist of what is necessary to achieve the goals can be helpful.

WHAT YOU CAN DO TO REVIEW SKILLS AND EXPERIENCE IN THE TEAM

Discuss in your team:

● What skills and experience are needed for this team to succeed?

● What skills and experience do we have now? What do we have too much or too little of?

● Who has too much or too little to do? Whose skills and experience are being under-utilised? Who is being overstretched?

● How could we rearrange the way we operate?

It is useful to consider too how the team manages changes in composition and how decisions are made about its size and the essential skills. The focus must be the job the team is there to do and how the members contribute to that. In cases of extreme overload, making representation for a new member may achieve results, once all other avenues have been explored. Replacing departing colleagues will be more effective with good induction and an adequate handover. However, increasingly teams are becoming leaner and need to be more efficient. To do this without overstress requires a regular reappraisal of how the team is operating, to make the maximum use of the existing members.

DEPENDENCY RELATIONSHIPS

How the team members relate to each other in terms of their job demands is an important aspect of stress. Who depends on whom for what to do their job? How does the performance or delivery of one person help or hinder another in their work? Plotting a dependency or interrelationship chart (see p. 143) can help to identify and clarify the requirements we have of each other to ensure that members work together to move smoothly towards team goals. The chart can also isolate difficulties in terms of procedures, job allocation, office layout and communications.

**WHAT YOU CAN DO TO EXPLORE
DEPENDENCY RELATIONSHIPS IN YOUR TEAM**

● Draw a dependency or interrelationship chart,
marking in each circle the key people you depend on
to do your job

● You can show dependency both ways – those you
depend on and those who depend on you

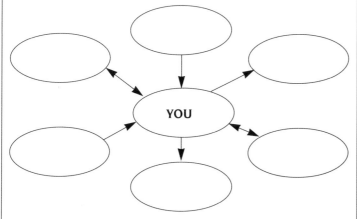

● You can also do this exercise to illustrate your team's
relationship with other teams in the organisation.
This may reveal the need for discussion and review of
procedures

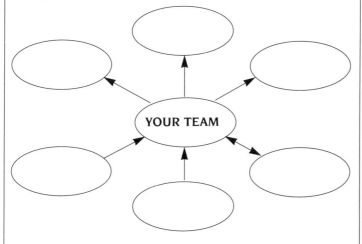

● Use the information in the dependency charts to
review the way you work and discuss this with the
relevant people

EVALUATION AND REVIEW

Does the team know how its performance is evaluated and by what criteria? Is it involved in the process of evaluation or is this carried out by someone outside the team? How is the information gained from the evaluation process used?

Knowing how we are doing, and having some part in the evaluation process, will extend influence and help reduce the powerlessness and unhealthy stress of unwelcome surprise/shock. In reviewing the team's performance it is important to take account of:

- near misses – when the team nearly achieved

- situations that changed beyond its control and affected performance, including new targets that were added

- how it worked, as well as what it achieved, to ensure that next time the team does even better.

WHAT YOU CAN DO TO EVALUATE AND REVIEW

Consider the following points with your team after completing a specific work project:

- How would you evaluate your performance as a team in that exercise?

- Did you achieve your targets or objectives?

- Did you work together constructively, using behaviour that was supportive? Give specific examples

- If relevant, how would you describe your working relationship with other teams?

- How did you overcome difficulties?

- What improvements could you have made?

- Were you an effective team?

MAKING TEAMS WORK

STAGES OF TEAM WORK

Often we expect teams to work effectively the moment they are established. However, groups generally move through stages. The following framework, developed from Tuckman (1965), can help in understanding the changes in the life of a team. Like most frameworks it should not be treated too rigidly, with the expectation that all stages will be experienced. However, teams that last for a long time are likely to have been through the stages several times.

Forming   the team meets for the first few times, establishes the task and its demands and explores what is involved in team membership. This can generate anxiety and uncertainty and consequently unhealthy stress.

Storming   usually the time when real differences of opinion and method become apparent, leading to conflict. Whilst overstress is often experienced, this can also be the greatest time for really learning to work together, particularly when differences have been faced, accepted and valued. It is then that realistic cooperation can be achieved and the strengths of individual members used to best effect so that positive stress can be generated and used constructively. Failure to work through this stage will affect the team's subsequent performance.

Norming   people develop an agreed way of getting on together with the task in hand, usually generating healthy stress.

Performing   builds on previous stages. Team members are likely to be in the Peaks, producing work of a high quality.

Mourning   often avoided or considered unnecessary, particularly in a culture where expression of feelings is thought to be suspect. However, if attention is not paid to the winding up of a team or the departure of a member , feelings that individuals have no opportunity to express can become destructive. Celebrations when tasks have been achieved or wakes to mourn the dispersal of members – or both together(!) – leave individuals with a more satisfactory and rounded experience of working in a team. There is then a likelihood that people will be willing to work effectively in one again.

By appreciating the stages through which a team is likely to move and the potential for healthy and unhealthy stress at each stage, we can manage the situation more productively. The alleviation of existing problems and the avoidance of new ones will be greatly enhanced by open and direct communication, which relies on procedures and skills in the team and positive attitudes to people. Essentially these are linked: procedures and skills will not bring about powerful relationships – they need the underpinnings of respect and regard for self and others. Only then will healthy stress result.

COOPERATION OR COMPETITION

The extent to which teams work cooperatively or in competition will reflect the culture of the organisation as well as the preferences of the team members and the norms that have developed. Whilst it can be argued that competition is healthy and leads to greater individual achievement, another view is that competition between team members can be destructive and directs energy away from the real competition – outside the organisation. Competitive behaviour, by its very nature, promotes winners and losers: this can create overstress and limit supportive team work. The challenge is to maintain a competitive edge in the market place whilst working cooperatively in the team.

The skills of cooperation do not come naturally. If at school we were taught that sharing is cheating and that the independent result is the only valuable one, then we will need to learn new approaches. The cooperative team will ensure that it is the team that wins, and will support its members to help them cope with their pressures.

Example: Patrick

Patrick worked in the fund-raising department of a charity. The team members needed to work cooperatively, sharing information and supporting each other in their difficult and demanding roles. Unfortunately, each person's performance was appraised against his or her individual achievements and not against the achievements of the team as a whole. This meant that they competed for recognition and did not achieve their expected success. The team work that would have generated results had been discouraged.

BUILDING RESPECT

We have probably at some time witnessed a team climate that is hostile or antagonistic, sulky or seething; where looks speak volumes but we cannot always pin down what is going on. These are teams where disagreements are not dealt with, and where the behaviour is characterised by power-play, put-downs and point-scoring. If we wish to form a team that acts as a support to its members, both in times of extreme pressure and in building up resistance to unhealthy stress, then we need relationships that confirm team members and convey value to them.

Positive relationships with all team members, regardless of personal likes and dislikes, stem from attitudes of respect for others. The ways in which we behave with each other communicate attitudes – of respect, indifference, disrespect, genuine interest or mere going through the motions of courtesy. We pick up messages through others' behaviour, both in terms of what they say and also in their non-verbal behaviour. As the non-verbal behaviour contains the emotional dimension of the message this is significant in suggesting their attitude towards us. Research has shown that we are particularly responsive to non-verbal signals, believing them rather than the words spoken if there is a mismatch.

One of the most basic of our needs is to be liked. Of course we are not paid to be liked, yet teams characterised by behaviour of mutual respect and support tend to be the most stress fit. They are also often the most productive and stimulating, for people feel safe to take risks. They can try new approaches, take new challenges, and feel that they will still be valued even if the outcome is not as was planned. In addition, these teams will become great places to work!

The self-esteem and confidence level of each team member is a crucial factor in this and will be influenced by job skills, work situation, and whether particular strengths are being utilised and work needs met. Understanding and valuing difference in the team are important parts of this.

Understanding the work demands of each individual, and finding ways to meet targets through team working, will do much to communicate respect and support and thus boost self-esteem. This will build up a solid base of confidence from which the team can grow to greater achievement. Low esteem can be exacerbated by role conflict and underachievement and this will affect interactions as well as job performance. By identifying what each can and does contribute to the team, we can build greater understanding of each person's skills and build the team. Teams that develop procedures to maximise each individual's input will feel more in control and stress fit.

WHAT YOU CAN DO TO BUILD A TEAM

- For each team member write on a large sheet of paper

  - your main skills

  - your strengths

  - your achievements in this job

  - your personal work goals

- Share these with the team, other members adding, confirming and giving examples

  - With which items does each member feel more and least confident?

  - How can greater use be made of skills and strengths in the team?

  - How can confidence be boosted? Through doing what? By what support?

  - How can personal work goals and challenges be met to generate healthy stress? Agree a plan of action for specific goals and tasks

---

AGREEING A FRAMEWORK FOR ACTION

It is useful to relate behaviour in teams to the expectations of each team member of the others and of the team. Bringing these expectations into the open can prove beneficial as views are expressed and explored and a shared view agreed or compromised on. For example, the team may agree that it is important to allow people to set their own work priorities, but that these must be communicated to others and take into account the team's priorities and interrelationships. Or it could be thought that resentments should be aired, and that people can express their views, but this will be done in a way that does not undermine others' esteem or feelings. Discussing beliefs, as explored in Chapter 5, can help in this process, as will agreeing a framework for action in the team.

WHAT YOU CAN DO WITH YOUR TEAM TO AGREE A FRAMEWORK FOR ACTION

First:

- Using your experience, both past and present, brainstorm all the things that you have disliked about working in teams

Then:

- Using this list as a starting point, discuss your ideas for effective working in this team. What behaviours are acceptable? What are not acceptable? What makes you feel good? What makes you feel annoyed?

From this:

- Generate a list of beliefs and expectations that the team members hold for themselves and for each other. The lists in Chapter 5 ('Creating a personal stress code') can provide a starting point. Relate these to behaviour. E.g. if a belief is that people can express views that are different from other people's, what behaviour will communicate and confirm this belief?

- Discuss: What values does this team subscribe to? How do they manifest themselves?

Finally:

- Make two lists of behaviours that people will try to avoid and behaviours that you will try to do more of, e.g.:

  Not interrupting others while speaking

  Showing you are listening by eye contact and head nods

- Using the lists, agree a framework for action and practise the behaviours!

- Discuss how you will let someone know if their behaviour strays into the unacceptable list. Teams can often generate light and humorous ways of doing this that are also acceptable to everyone

**DEVELOPING AN ASSERTIVE
TEAM**

Assertive behaviour expresses the person's feelings, attitudes, wishes, opinions or beliefs directly, firmly and honestly, while respecting those of the other person. It may include the expression of feelings such as annoyance, fear, hope, pleasure, indignation or embarrassment, but in a manner that does not violate the rights of others.

By developing the skills of assertion in each team member we can move towards developing an assertive team. Sometimes we need to be assertive to ensure that our views are heard and our needs are met. As we learn to influence the workings of the team, we build up a greater sense of belonging and commitment to the team and its goals.

The exercises in this chapter will already have led us some way towards assertiveness as they explore its underpinnings: our expectations of each other and beliefs about relationships. In assertive teams, power is shared amongst the members. Each one is seen as being as valuable and important as the others, and feels confident enough of his or her own worth for it not to be dependent on others. In such teams all views are valued, even if they are not acted upon; the goals are never lost sight of, whilst the factors that interfere in their achievement are acknowledged and responded to.

An assertive team will take control of the way it works, will tackle difficult situations, will strive to create the appropriate stress conditions and will say 'no' to unhealthy stress.

WHAT YOU CAN DO TO RESOLVE PROBLEM SITUATIONS IN AN ASSERTIVE WAY

- State your position firmly and clearly. Use 'I' messages and make a clear statement of your feelings

- Use active listening to hear the other person's position and feelings. Check that you have understood

- Empathise. Reflect back to the other person what they have just said, demonstrating that you understand their viewpoint and can appreciate their feelings

- Negotiate. Discuss possible solutions to the problem, listening to the other person and putting forward ideas.

- Be prepared to compromise – find a solution that satisfies both parties at least partially

- State this solution clearly so that you both understand and accept it

- Remember that there are some things that you might not wish to compromise on. In these situations make your position understood by stating it clearly and assertively. This does not mean that you have to be aggressive.

With the best will in the world, there will be times when resentments are felt, anger or irritation experienced or disagreement rife. These are the times when the fight/flight/freeze responses often take over. If we feel uncomfortable with the situation, and are unsure of the best way to tackle it, we may go silent and avoid the situation, speak in rather general terms and back down if pressed, talk to others about the problem but not the person involved or use the sort of behaviour, verbal or non-verbal, designed to get the other person thinking they are at fault, such as sulking or sarcasm. All of these behaviours infect others with the stress virus and they avoid confrontation of the issues, which might just resolve the situation. Confrontation can actually be extremely positive and productive if tackled assertively and with care, so that no one is a total loser in the situation.

One key to effective handling of disagreement is the recognition that it can be valuable. If we all agreed with each other, it is unlikely that we could move towards creative solutions. As teams are composed of differences we need to accept and welcome conflict and disagreement, viewing it as a resource for creativity and enhanced effectiveness, provided we handle it effectively. We can develop some simple procedures to help us do this.

DEALING WITH CONFLICT AND DISAGREEMENT

WHAT YOU CAN DO TO DEAL WITH CONFLICT AND DISAGREEMENTS

- View conflict as valuable. Although it may feel uncomfortable, it is necessary for a successful team

- As with any strong feeling, an honest expression of what you are feeling, acknowledged by others, can often be all that is needed to minimise the discomfort

cont.

- Related to this is how we respond to the expression of others' feelings: listening skills are essential here. Recognising that we are not responsible for others' feelings will help our response

- It is also helpful to check your understanding of what has been said by reflecting back the key points you have just heard

- Keeping your voice as neutral as possible and your body language as relaxed as you can will help communicate your message clearly. Similarly, when receiving a disagreeing view, try not to react to any emotion in the voice or behaviour, but listen and respond to the words

- Acknowledge the validity of the other person's view, even if you do not agree with it. They are entitled to their view

- Sometimes it is necessary to agree to differ. This can still be done in an atmosphere of respect and warmth for each other

PATTERNS OF COMMUNICATION

Given the links between stress and communication and control, reviewing the communication practices, both formal and informal, within the team can reveal areas to change or develop.

CHECKLIST: TEAM COMMUNICATION

In their daily work routines:

How do individuals communicate?

- Do they talk face to face?

- Do they talk on the telephone?

- Do they rely on memos and messages?

- How often does the team meet?

- Are there procedures for briefing and keeping in touch?

What do they talk about?

- Work demands and requests?

- 'How to' discussions?

- Ideas for projects or approaches?

- Personal information, e.g. feelings, experiences, either related to the situation or not?

- Social matters and personal life?

How are decisions made?

- Are opinions asked?

- Is advice given?

- Are decisions made together?

How effectively do individuals communicate?

- Do they listen and respond to each other?

- Do the body language and spoken language match?

- Are underlying issues picked up and discussed?

- Do they have strategies for dealing with conflict or disagreement or are they viewed as unproductive or threatening?

- Are leadership and chairing of projects or meetings in the most appropriate hands? Are they shared or rotated?

- Who 'owns' decisions?

Does the team review progress and achievements?

- Who monitors performance and how?

- Are individual achievements and near-misses valued and shared as well as the team's?

- Does the team learn from failure and celebrate success?

WHAT YOU CAN DO TO IMPROVE PATTERNS OF COMMUNICATION

Using the checklist above:

- Review individually and then discuss with your team which aspects of your current practice cause dissatisfaction and potential pressure

- Consider what would make things better

- Agree and draft an action plan for each team member as a result

- Monitor and review progress regularly

WHAT YOU CAN DO TO ESTABLISH A POSITIVE CLIMATE

In your team, brainstorm then discuss:

- What makes this team special?

- What do you like about working in this team?

Organisational Stress 10

Just as individuals and teams will develop habits of responding to pressure, so organisations show characteristics of how they manage and respond to stress.

There are two extremes of this organisational relationship with stress. At one end of the scale the stress virus gets passed around, with people who experience it creating more overstress by their reactions, until there is an epidemic. Anyone who is unable to keep up with the pressure is considered to be a weak link who does not measure up to the standards expected in such a hard environment. This eventually leads to the survival of the fittest and toughest, who ensure that new appointees are in their own image. A great deal of commitment, talent and ability may well be wasted in the process. In this climate overstress becomes endemic in the workplace and, while this may prove highly effective and productive in the short term, the long-term implications will be lowering of output, growing absenteeism and greater turnover of staff.

The dangers here are immense as unhealthy stress leads to inefficiency, loss of morale and reduced performance. With its links with illness, physical and mental, it is an occupational hazard. In fact in the USA there has been a spate of legal actions against organisations that cause undue workplace stress. US workers' compensation claims related to stress tripled during the first half of the 1980s, which suggests that the organisation's role in creating unhealthy stress is being taken seriously.

AVOIDING THE EXTREMES

At the other end of the scale are the organisations where people are understressed. These too are less than effective, perhaps achieving a measure of success but never reaching great heights. They are often vulnerable to rapid changes in the economic, social and political environment in which they operate. They will also be losing out on the potential of their employees, who will not have the opportunities to be appropriately challenged and developed. Where this occurs there will be frustration and a high turnover of able staff, who will be going to other organisations where they can progress.

There is sometimes a stress blockage where overstress is locked in at a certain level in the organisation. For instance, managers may all be verging on the stress Spiral but their staff are being under-used. This can be because there is an underestimation of the capacity of the staff or because effective delegation is not part of a manager's training. This is yet another way of wasting people's potential.

Example: A union

A large union conducted a survey on causes of stress in the workplace. It was discovered that there was overstress in some areas of management but understress in others where the staff were not having work delegated to them that they could easily have done. As a result of the findings the union has appointed a full-time welfare officer who is using an external employee assistance programme (more about these later in the chapter); she has installed a health screening programme and is planning other strategies to see that pressure is spread round the organisation more appropriately.

While there is no legal obligation on organisations in Britain to monitor stress levels, the Health and Safety Commission's *Management of Health and Safety at Work – Approved Code of Practice* (1992) makes some helpful statements. Although the Code is mainly concerned with physical risks and hazards, it includes 'work processes and work organisation' as factors in assessing risks to health and safety at work. It also recommends 'medical surveillance, which may include clinical examination and measurements of physiological and psychological effects by an appropriately qualified practitioner' where suitable. The psychological aspect is included for the first time, but both areas are relevant to stress management.

Too often in the past stress management has been considered to be the individual's responsibility. But increasingly organisations are understanding how managing stress can have a pay-off for them as well as their employees, by moving away from stress virus epidemics towards stress fitness.

Example: An insurance company
One large insurance company has an impressive array of questionnaires and handouts about stress for the stress management module on their management development programme. The material addresses managers, teams and individuals.

Over 91 per cent of the organisations that responded to the Industrial Society survey were already engaged in good practice, perhaps for reasons other than stress management, but each activity contributes to an environment in which stress fitness is possible.

ORGANISATIONAL STRESS CHECK

If good stress management practices are to be effective and used as a matter of course, there needs to be an overall commitment from the highest levels. If this happens then the subject is more likely to be taken seriously by all employees, most importantly by those who influence decisions that affect working practices. This is particularly true where a change in attitudes and behaviour is required, as was revealed in research by the Ashridge Management Research Group for the Opportunity 2000 project, which aims to improve the balance of men and women in the workplace (Hammond and Holton, 1991).

SHARING THE RESPONSIBILITY

THE OVERALL VIEW

WHAT YOU CAN DO TO RAISE AWARENESS OF STRESS AS A SERIOUS ISSUE

- Express commitment to managing stress at the highest possible level

- Raise stress as an issue at management meetings and get people talking about its positive and negative effects

- Nominate a senior manager to oversee and coordinate activities

- Provide regular medical checks

cont.

- Ensure that staff take all their annual leave, with at least one two-week break where possible

- Discourage any signs of a 'long hours' culture at all levels

- Conduct a programme of research (either formally or informally) into effects of stress in the workplace and act on the findings

POLICY STATEMENT

Unless organisations take a clear stand on the issue of stress management, any actions by individuals to tackle the problem will have limited effect, particularly given the inhibitions about raising the topic. As one respondent to the Industrial Society survey expressed it, 'Whatever the strength of the argument, the issue just would not be taken seriously in my organisation as it's just not macho'!

It is helpful if there is a written policy statement about the management of stress at work; this might be part of a health policy that all employees should know about. A senior manager should have responsibility for making sure that the policy is implemented. This person would see that there were ways of monitoring stress levels and of removing any unnecessary causes of unhealthy stress. There would also need to be resources and opportunities for helping both the organisation and the employee to take steps to improve the situation.

ICL, a computer company, makes its position clear in an Occupational Health Policy statement. It is the policy of the group 'to ensure that the health of employees is not adversely affected by their work or working environment and to promote a healthy lifestyle among employees'. In its focus on stress-related problems, it identifies that the cost to the organisation can be very high.

> The precipitating factor which causes a deterioration in an individual's performance may be obscure and is often unrelated to work. However, managers need to be aware that it is often far more cost effective to modify the individual's work temporarily than to continue to apply pressure which may lead to a complete breakdown in health.

> The real cost of implementing a policy will be reduced by taking into account the potential impact on the organisation of

unhealthy stress, and by taking proactive steps to ensure that managers are aware of and can implement the organisation's approach to the issue.

WHAT YOU CAN DO TO DEVELOP A STRESS POLICY

- Include in a stress policy statement:

  The organisation's commitment to:
  - managing stress effectively
  - fully utilising the potential of employees
  - enabling employees to maintain good health whilst meeting their job demands

  A *recognition of*:
  - the links between performance and stress as well as organisational culture and stress
  - the cost to the organisation of unhealthy stress
  - the potential for the manager to aggravate the situation by carelessly applying extra pressure

  The importance of:
  - monitoring performance
  - recognising the symptoms of unhealthy stress
  - acting promptly on stress problems uncovered
  - counselling skills and stress coaching

  Communication of any additional policies or procedures such as:
  - the circumstances in which a problem should be referred on and how to do so
  - the supports available, such as an employee assistance programme (see later in the chapter), welfare service or occupational health service

- Develop a plan to implement the policy

- Make sure that the policy is communicated clearly to all employees

- Ensure that they have the skills and resources required to implement it

- Monitor the implementation

- Promote good health in words and deeds!

STRUCTURE

Organisational structure can cause unnecessary stress.

Is the structure of your organisation, whether hierarchical or horizontal, appropriate to its aims?   Structures often have their roots in history but may no longer be suitable for modern working practices or present-day conditions.

Are there the appropriate number of hierarchical levels? There can be too many or too few, and recent trends have often involved the removal of a whole tier of management. This may ultimately make the organisation more flexible but can cause overstress in the process.

Are responsibility and decision-making at the most appropriate level?   Accountability is being spread nowadays but it is essential that those who undertake responsibility and make decisions have the skills and the powers to do so.

Is team working used where appropriate?   Some projects are best handled by a short-term or longer-term team.

How is change managed?   Whether change results from external circumstances or from internal reorganisation, there may be a short-term risk of overstress from the change itself.

MANAGEMENT STYLES

Stress factors are involved in whatever management style prevails in an organisation because they affect relationships.

Does the management style achieve the appropriate balance between consultation and control?   Managers help develop cooperative working by consulting but must be ready and able to take the ultimate decisions and be accountable for them.

Where work is delegated, are enough training and support given and is the effect on stress levels monitored?   It is no good giving a job to someone who is not clear about what is expected or who is already fully stretched.

Are people doing similar work in the organisation all being equally utilised or do the 'willing people' tend to receive greater workloads?   A great deal of dissatisfaction among staff can be avoided by paying attention to this point.

COMMUNICATION

One of the main complaints on courses on stress management is lack of communication.

Does enough information flow in every appropriate direction to the right people at the right time?   Policy changes, new ideas and complaints, among other things, need to reach the person or people who can deal with them in good time.

Is the most suitable method used for disseminating information?   Consider whether word of mouth, a team briefing, the telephone, a fax, a memo, a letter or an article in the company magazine is the most appropriate way to reach the person or people who either need to know or would be interested.

Employment practices can help to reduce unhealthy stress in many ways, but they are often the cause themselves when carried out insensitively.

EMPLOYMENT PRACTICE

If there are career paths, are they made explicit to all employees?   Opportunities for developing able staff are often lost because they do not know what is required and are not encouraged to apply for training or promotion.

Are employees consulted about decisions that affect their careers?   Ultimately people are individually responsible for their own lives and can become overstressed if they feel they have no control over what is happening to them.

Do you offer the appropriate training for people to make them more effective and develop their careers?   Training can be offered within the company but there are times when it is more effective or expedient when provided from outside.

Have the benefits and the costs (not just monetary) been considered when deciding on long- or short-term employment?   Short-term contracts will make the organisation more flexible but may lose commitment from the employees, particularly those who are career-minded. There is added pressure because of the uncertainty about whether the contract will be renewed. Long-term employment may lead to complacency, but the organisation can reap the benefits of experience and loyalty.

Are there opportunities for employees to manage flexible career paths that are appropriate to their stress needs?
There are times in people's lives when they cannot cope with more responsibility, at least for the time being. This is not always acceptable in firms that see this as a lack of the required attitude. As a consequence people may push themselves, or be pushed into, positions that they cannot manage and find themselves on the stress Spiral.

Do you offer leave or career breaks for family commitments

without this affecting career prospects for the individual?
A great deal of unnecessary stress is avoided where there are clear policies for all staff who have family commitments, whether for children, elderly relatives or disabled dependants.

Do you offer job-sharing as a way of keeping good staff?
This needs some careful management but can be extremely effective.

Do you offer help with childcare arrangements?   Many organisations find that these can help to keep good staff who might otherwise have to leave. Creches can reduce stress levels in parents, particularly when they are near enough for them to respond in an emergency.

Do you have an equal opportunities policy that is well monitored?   A great deal of unhealthy stress can be avoided by making clear that responsibility lies with everyone to make sure that there is no discrimination based on race, gender, age or disability. There need to be systems that are known to everyone to back this up, and a senior manager responsible for seeing that they work.

Are there systems to deal with sexual or racial harassment?
Everybody needs to know what to do if harassment occurs and that it will be handled sensitively, discreetly and effectively.

Do you have an appraisal scheme?   Such schemes need to make sure that there is an opportunity to discuss the appraisee's achievements as well as possible improvements. There should also be time for discussing training needs and possible career development. There should be the possibility for appraisees to talk about anything else in their life that may be affecting them, but this needs to be handled sensitively. Information should be able to flow between the interviewer and the interviewee. If the appraisal scheme is related to promotion or pay, there is less likelihood of the appraisee being able to discuss difficulties freely. The appraiser should not, of course, limit a show of interest to an annual appraisal but should be aware of what is happening to the appraisee and offering support throughout the year. When people know where they stand they will feel less unhealthily stressed. Upward appraisal is needed too.

Are people valued regularly for their contributions?   One of the best ways of reducing stress levels is to make sure that efforts are rewarded (not necessarily financially) by paying tribute to good work. All people appreciate being valued.

How are disputes handled on both an organisational and

an individual level?   Clearly industrial relations need to be
managed by people who are competent to do so. More often,
though, it is relationships between individuals that can become
stressful. How to handle conflict needs to be included in training
programmes so that the creative use of it can be enhanced and
the people involved can find ways of making sure that each
person wins something from the dispute, however small. If
friction is ignored it can very easily activate the stress virus.

JOB DESIGN

Resources spent in this area can help to give people some
security in what they are doing.

Do you have clear job descriptions?   These should be
agreed by the person holding the post and leave possibilities
for development if appropriate. In entrepreneurial positions
the job description may need to be open ended, but everyone
needs to know what their goals are and what targets they are
expected to reach.
**Is care taken to make sure that people have the right skills,
qualities, experience and training to carry out their jobs
effectively?**   Many people are left to sink or swim in
organisations when a little care would help them to be better
contributors to the workplace.
Are roles clarified either formally or informally?   Role
conflict and ambiguity contribute greatly to unhealthy stress.

WORKPLACE ENVIRONMENT

Physical surroundings have been extensively researched with
relation to stress in the workplace.

**Do you fulfil all the requirements of the health and safety
legislation?**   This is being constantly revised, particularly now
to bring it into line with the European Community regulations.
People must know what the rules are and how to implement
them.
**Are heating, lighting, ventilation, noise, furniture and space
constantly being monitored?**   People need to be consulted
about these issues since it is not always possible to imagine
what a work situation is like for another person. Taking care
over the employees' environment is a way of showing that
people are being valued, and if they feel that they can influence
improvements then they will be more in control of their lives.
**Has consideration been given to travelling conditions for
employees?**   Travelling to and from work or travelling as part
of the job can be a source of overstress. Ease of access and

transport facilities are important considerations when planning to set up a new workplace.

Is there adequate parking space for those who need it?
Disputes over parking often contribute to overstress in already busy people. Those who travel as part of the job or who live in places that lack adequate public transport can be helped by good parking facilities or transport laid on by the organisation. Where there is little that can be done to improve things, provision should be made for people to relax after a bad journey before they settle down to work.

WHAT YOU CAN DO TO CONDUCT AN ORGANISATIONAL STRESS CHECK
● Use the questions in this section to identify those areas that you need to tackle and the actions that you need to take

SUPPORTS

Organisations do many things to provide supports for stress management.

TRAINING

Nearly 72 per cent of the respondents to the Industrial Society survey offered **job-related training and development**. Apart from the practical benefits, this has the added benefit of giving people knowledge and skills so that they do not feel uncertain, ill-equipped or out of control, which could induce unhealthy stress. However, training people to do their jobs will not in itself help them to handle their stress more effectively or prevent the spread of the stress virus.

Another aspect of training that is increasingly being seen as important for managers is the development of **counselling skills**, which can help a manager to address the problem of unhealthy stress among staff and to find ways of relieving it. By active listening, appropriate questioning, reflecting back what has been said to check if it has been understood correctly and generally offering support when needed (as outlined in 'What You Can Do to Stress Coach' in Chapter 8), the manager can show concern for what is happening to a member of staff. Even if it is not possible to sort out a particular difficulty, or the staff member is unwilling to discuss it with someone who holds disciplinary and promotional power, the manager can at least help to find appropriate help and support.

To be effective in using these skills the manager or superviser needs to have an underlying respect for individuals and their right to be responsible for their own lives and decisions.

With problems that demand greater expertise and time than may be available, referral to a counselling service will be necessary.

Example: A brewery

A stress survey for a brewery found overstress at all levels of the organisation, with the worst levels being on the shop floor. It is now implementing the recommendations made and is:

– reviewing communication systems

– training people to recognise stress in themselves and what to do about it

– training managers to recognise stress in others and what action to take

– helping its occupational health staff to develop counselling skills so that employees have someone to share their worries with and get some support

Courses to improve people's **assertiveness** can help them to grow in confidence and take opportunities to contribute more fully to the organisation. Being assertive can also make it more likely that people will develop their full potential and avoid frustration. Over 20 per cent of the organisations in the Industrial Society survey ran assertiveness programmes.

At the end of people's careers, good preparation in the form of **pre-retirement courses** will help people to maintain morale as retirement approaches and also to manage the stress involved in the change of lifestyle. This kind of appreciation of the work that they have done over the years can make them feel that it was worth while and that they are not just being dumped on the scrap heap. The subjects that need planning for are finances, time management, activities, health care and relationships after they have left the organisation.

STRESS MANAGEMENT TRAINING

It was encouraging to find that nearly one-third of those replying to the Industrial Society survey were offering stress management training programmes and/or included stress management within their management development programmes.

Example: An insurance company
One insurance company offers stress management workshops and has produced an excellent booklet covering the main issues as well as ideas for helping. It also provides an audio cassette that outlines relaxation techniques. Stress management is covered on its retirement courses.

An important first step is to recognise that unnecessary demands and constraints can interfere with employees' meeting their job demands. So feedback from training courses that is then acted on can do a great deal to reduce unnecessary stress. However, this is often not encouraged because the information may well add more pressure to already overstressed managers!

WHAT YOU CAN INCLUDE IN A STRESS MANAGEMENT TRAINING PROGRAMME

- A working definition of stress, including the different types of stress: understress, healthy stress and overstress

- Consideration of the healthy and unhealthy effects of stress and the shared responsibility for stress at work

- The stress virus

- Identification of causes of pressure both in and out of work

- Typical responses to stress, including those in the body, thoughts, feelings and actions

- How to recognise unhealthy stress in oneself and others

- Practical strategies that individuals can adopt to manage stress in themselves and others, and to keep in the Peaks

- Ways to incorporate an understanding of stress into the management process

- Skills to help all of the above (as outlined in the book)

WELFARE SERVICES

Many organisations that responded to the Industrial Society survey already have occupational health services. Others arrange for health screening on a regular basis. In fact some of the doctors involved wished that their employers would take the subject seriously and make it possible to improve both management practices and support systems for employees. At the same time, many realised the benefits of healthy stress.

COUNSELLING

Counselling skills, as described earlier in the chapter, will help people to deal with others effectively. But when someone needs concentrated help, perhaps over a period of time, then other supports may be needed. Professional counselling is a useful resource in this respect.

Counselling comes in many forms but basically offers an individual the opportunity to talk about, examine and work out a way of improving a situation for themselves. Even though there may not be a neat solution, during the process of exploring the circumstances more understanding is achieved and symptoms of unhealthy stress are usually relieved. In fact in some research undertaken in the Post Office by Cooper, Sadri, Allison and Reynolds in 1990 it was discovered that, by introducing a stress counselling service, sickness absence was reduced by 66 per cent. This clearly saved a great deal of money as well as improving the mental well-being, self-esteem and stress fitness of postal workers.

Example: A manufacturing company

The occupational health doctor in a manufacturing company refers people to professional counsellors, particularly when they are suffering from anxiety or depression, both of which may have a relationship with stress.

A fully trained counsellor will have had at least two years part-time training, and provides a caring, non-judgemental environment and support to aid the process of self-understanding. The information discussed will be treated as confidential and trust will be built up so that the person who is troubled can talk freely about themselves.

People are often 'sent to be counselled', but this will not be successful if the person does not want to be counselled. This is why emphasis is always put on people referring themselves to a counsellor.

WHAT YOU CAN DO TO FIND OUT MORE ABOUT COUNSELLING

- Contact the British Association for Counselling, which has a division for counselling at work, at:

  BAC
  1 Regent Place
  Rugby
  Warwickshire CV21 2PJ   Tel: 0788 578328

EMPLOYEE ASSISTANCE PROGRAMMES

This is one of the ways of investing in an organisation's most valuable asset – its employees. EAPs have been described as 'counselling programmes in organisational settings'. Those who offer them can provide a wide range of services that are intended to care for employees and their families where problems are becoming unmanageable. These may include targeting particular problem areas (for instance alcohol abuse), and may also provide information, assessment, referral and counselling services.

Example: A transport service

A region of one transport service has introduced an EAP that gives basic training in counselling skills to some carefully picked members of the permanent staff. This service is backed up by support from the EAP organisation.

Mike Megranahan (1990) considers the following features to be essential if an employee assistance programme is to be effective:

- the support of top management

- a written company statement of overall philosophy and policy concerning the health and well-being of its employees, which should express its positive attitude towards persons who seek professional assistance for psychological or emotional problems

- supervisors who can assess job performance problems and help subordinates to recognize these problems

- the support of the union or other employee representatives

- a professional diagnostic component to the programme to help employees to assess their problems

- a continuum of care, which includes referral and follow-up

- evaluation of the programme

- an emphasis on promoting self-referrals, not relying solely on supervisory referrals

- a high level of confidentiality

- a service which should be available to all employees and dependants

- an appropriate employee benefit package – most especially health coverage

---

WHAT YOU CAN DO TO FIND OUT MORE ABOUT EAPS

● Contact the Employee Assistance Professionals Association at:

EAPA
Wyvals Court
Swallowsfield
Reading
Berks RG7 1PY   Tel: 0734 880218

One way of helping employees to manage their stress more effectively is to encourage a healthy lifestyle and physical fitness. Actively promoting the value of being fit for the job has the effect of setting norms of expected behaviour, for example a work-out in the gym or a swim in the pool rather than a pint in the bar or a local pub. Such an approach to stress management is proving increasingly popular and nearly 53 per

FIT FOR WORK

cent of respondents to the Industrial Society survey used sporting and leisure facilities to promote a healthy lifestyle.

As has been identified in Chapter 7, physical exercise is vital in avoiding the unhealthy physical consequences of overstress. Exercising uses up the extra fats released into the bloodstream when responding to pressure. At times of high pressure a sense of proportion is easier to maintain if people are physically fit. It also helps to give people a measure of control over their lives.

Providing facilities, or access to facilities, for sport and leisure has the potential added benefit of communicating to the workforce a sense that they are valued and that their welfare is of concern. This will help to build loyalty and commitment as well as providing cost benefits.

It is important to review the refreshments available to people during the working day. A constant supply of coffee and tea will not help stress management. Company policies on smoking and the consumption of alcohol will also be relevant here.

WHAT YOU CAN DO TO DEVELOP A HEALTHY WORKFORCE

- Consider ways of providing sporting facilities if they are not already available

- For information, contact the Sports Council:
  16 Upper Woburn Place
  London WCl OQP   Tel: 071 388 1277

- If you have a canteen and/or provide refreshments and drinks in breaks, review the choices on offer. Make sure they are not all caffeine rich, fat full and sugar laden. Provide healthy drinks, including herb teas, fruit juices and good-quality fresh water, high-quality healthy snacks and meals with fresh fruit, vegetables and salads

- Discourage smoking at work and drinking alcohol during the working day

---

SOCIAL EVENTS

As has been discussed in Chapter 7, many aspects of life need to be taken into account if people are to be stress fit. Socialising can be helpful in many ways in reducing unhealthy stress. It can help people to see each other as whole people, with interests outside work and, even if some of the talk may be about work, it can give people opportunities of letting off steam with others who understand.

It would be helpful to begin by finding out whether a social club or social activities would be welcome, and of what kind.

It may seem ironic to suggest that organisations should offer employees ways of relaxing; we hope that by this stage in the book it is understood that, to be stress fit, it is necessary to have real breaks from work from time to time. If these are to be truly effective they must be well thought out. Congenial canteens, rest rooms and pleasant grounds outside, where possible, all help people to get even a few minutes relief if the pressure is high.

Whilst only 7 per cent of the respondents to the Industrial Society survey provided relaxation programmes, press coverage of other organisations suggests that this is one of the most newsworthy aspects of stress management. Massage and Alexander technique classes for employees of the *Independent* newspaper, a visiting masseur in the City and meditation sessions at the Mountain Breeze company are just some of the more recent examples. Learning to relax helps in long-term stress management and developing stress fitness. It also has clear health benefits for the individual.

WHAT YOU CAN DO TO EDUCATE FOR RELAXATION

- Look for ways to promote the benefits of relaxation or provide relaxation classes for all employees
- Provide relaxing environments for breaks

ORGANISATIONAL STRESS FITNESS

Addressing the organisational culture and how it is communicated is central to achieving stress fitness. It is not only what we say about stress, but whether our actions reinforce or contradict the public statements, that will convince others that we mean what we say. As one respondent to the Industrial Society survey said, 'stress is a widely recognised business issue, yet few (seemingly) employers devote resources to addressing the problem'. Perhaps this is because stress is frequently not recognised by the managers, other than in

themselves!

Encouraging a balanced approach to work, in which the importance of free time and leisure activities is emphasized, will help to build a stress-fit organisation made up of stress-fit individuals. What is essential is training in the views, attitudes and practices of such a workforce, and the development of stress management skills.

Example: A manufacturing company

A well-known manufacturing company has a trained counsellor who has a written policy on the confidential service he offers. He has produced an excellent booklet with amusing illustrations, more than half of which consist of suggestions for managing stress. The company also has a 'Whole Health Programme', which offers:

- a smoking policy

- a policy on healthy eating

- a heart health check

- counselling

- courses on:
  - stress management
  - relaxation skills
  - alcohol awareness
  - assertiveness training

- exercise facilities:
  - a sports and social club
  - an annual 10km and fun run.

Clearly a great deal of thought and care have been put into making sure that the employees are stress fit.

In an Apple/Henley survey (1990), the ability to manage change was identified by 33 per cent of chief executives as the most important attribute for successful companies to have in the next five years. Changes generate stress, both healthy and unhealthy. As organisations confront and implement the changes that will mean the difference between success or failure, survival or extinction, they will have to recognise that their future performance will be dramatically affected by the way they learn to manage and, it is hoped, thrive on stress.

PART IV

RESOURCES

Further Information about Possible Supports

GENERAL

The Yellow Pages telephone directories will list many of the helpful agencies and practitioners in your area.

CITIZENS ADVICE BUREAUX

Most towns have a CAB, which has information about most of the helpful agencies in the area.

COMPLEMENTARY MEDICINE

There is now an Institute of Complementary Medicine that is concerned about standards of practitioners. Its register provides information about local practitioners and complementary therapies. Send an s.a.e. (plus three 1st class stamps, unused and unlicked, to help with their expenses) for information to:

The British Register of Complementary Practitioners
PO Box 194
London SE16 1QZ   Tel: 071 237 5165

ACUPUNCTURE

For information about acupuncturists who are also medical doctors contact:

The British Medical Acupuncture Society
Newton House
Newton Lane
Whitley

Warrington
Cheshire WA4 4JA   Tel: 0925 730727

For information about other acupuncturists send £2 to:

The Council for Acupuncture
179 Gloucester Place
London NW1 6DX   Tel: 081 724 5756

There is also:

The Traditional Acupuncture Society
1 The Ridgeway
Stratford upon Avon
Warwickshire CV37 9LJ   Tel: 0789 298798

ALCOHOL AND DRUGS

Your local GP is likely to know what services are available in your area. Alternatively there are now Health Information Centres in each of the Health Authorities, giving information about any aspect of health, and there is a central telephone service where you can find out the most appropriate agency in your area:

Tel: 0800 665544

ALEXANDER TECHNIQUE

For information about the Alexander Technique and a list of their teachers send a large s.a.e. to:

The Society of Teachers of the Alexander Technique
20 London House
266 Fulham Rd
London SW10 9EL   Tel: 071 351 0828

AROMATHERAPY

Information from:

The International Federation of Aromatherapists
Royal Masonic Hospital
Ravenscourt Park
London W6 OTN   Tel: 081 846 8066

ASSERTIVENESS

Courses in assertiveness are run all over the country. The most effective ones will have a high proportion of skills practice. The local adult education centre will probably have information.

CHIROPRACTIC

You can get a list of chiropracters for £1 from:

The British Chiropractic Association

Premier House
10 Greycoat Place
London SW1 1SB   Tel: 071 222 8866

COUNSELLING

For general information and a list of counsellors send an s.a.e. to:

The British Association for Counselling
1 Regent Place
Rugby
Warwickshire CV21 2PJ   Tel: 0788 578328

The Westminster Pastoral Foundation offers counselling and psychotherapy at the following address, but also has accredited centres round the country:

The Westminster Pastoral Foundation
23 Kensington Square
London W8 5HN   Tel: 071 937 6956

Many organisations specialise in particular areas of human experience, two of which are:

For anyone with a difficulty in any kind of relationship:

Relate
Herbert Gray College
Little Church St
Rugby
Warwickshire CV21 3AP   Tel: 0788 573241

For anyone who has been bereaved:

Cruse
Cruse House
126 Sheen Rd
Richmond
Surrey TW9 1UR   Tel: 081 940 4818/9047

CRAFTS *See* **INTERESTS**

DRUGS *See* **ALCOHOL**

For information about diet, alcohol, caffeine, smoking, drugs and general health care contact:

HEALTH EDUCATION AUTHORITY

See The Health Education Authority
Hamilton House
Mabeldon Place
London WC1H 9TX   Tel: 071 383 3833

For information about fully trained homoeopaths send an s.a.e. to:

HOBBIES *See* INTERESTS

HOMEOPATHY

The Society of Homoeopaths
2 Artizan Rd
Northampton NN1 4HU   Tel: 0604 21400

or for information about medical doctors who also offer homoeopathy send an s.a.e. to:

The British Homoeopathic Association
27A Devonshire St
London WIN IRJ   Tel: 071 935 2163

Information from:

HYPNOTHERAPY

National College of Hypnosis and Psychotherapy
12 Cross St
Nelson
Lancashire BB9 7EN   Tel: 0282 699378

Most areas have local centres for adult education which run courses and classes in a whole range of subjects including crafts and hobbies. They are often attached to local schools, colleges or universities.

INTERESTS

Information from:

KINESIOLOGY

Association and Academy of Systematic Kinesiology
39 Browns Rd
Surbiton
Surrey KT5 8ST   Tel: 081 399 3215

Because there are so many different approaches to massage it may take a while to find one that suits you. Your local medical practice, a centre offering complementary therapies or your local library may be able to help you.

MASSAGE

For information about transcendental meditation and the courses they run send an s.a.e. to:

MEDITATION

Transcendental Meditation
FREEPOST
London SWI 4YY   Tel: 0800 269303

For information about other approaches to meditation read
Louis Proto's book *Meditation for Everybody*, published by Penguin.

OPEN UNIVERSITY

Most Open University courses are studied at home, supported
by tutorials and residential elements. Send an s.a.e for
information to:

> Central Enquiry Service
> PO Box 200
> Open University
> Milton Keynes MK7 6YX   Tel: 0908 653231

OSTEOPATHY

You can get a list of practitioners from:

> The General Council and Register of Osteopaths
> 56 London St
> Reading
> Berks RG1 4SQ   Tel: 0734 576585

REFLEXOLOGY

For information:

> The Association of Reflexologists
> 27 Old Gloucester St
> London WC1 3XX   Tel: 071 237 6523

SHIATSU

Send an s.a.e. for information to:

> The Shiatsu Society Administrator
> 14 Oakdene Rd
> Redhill
> Surrey RH1 6BT   Tel: 0737 767896

SPORTS

For information about sports centres or sports' governing
bodies in England send an s.a.e. (but check how much they
need to cover postage) to:

> Sports Council
> 16 Upper Woburn Place
> London WC1H OQP   Tel: 071 388 1277

RELAXATION *See* **THE
SECTION FOR SOME MORE
IDEAS**

There are separate sports councils for Wales, Scotland and
Northern Ireland and the local sports centres and governing
bodies will be able to give more detail about local facilities and
clubs. The local library will probably have a list of local clubs.

For information contact:

The British Wheel of Yoga
1 Hamilton Place
Boston Rd
Sleaford
Lincolnshire NG34 7ES   Tel: 0529 306851

Relaxation Exercises

These are some further exercises you can do to help with relaxing. Part of the aim of doing them regularly is to become aware of and release tension; part of the benefit is to concentrate the mind on something other than worries and work. They will need more time than the ones described in 'Relaxation on the Run', and a quiet, comfortable, uninterrupted place in some cases. It takes some practice to be able to do these exercises really effectively, so do not give up too soon!

(1) Take a few deep breaths. While you are doing this, try to think that you are filling your lungs with liquid air so that they fill from the bottom up, until they are completely full. When you breathe out, think about squeezing the air out from the bottom of your lungs first until every bit is pushed out. (If you find that you are feeling dizzy or your fingers are tingling this means that you are taking too much air in, so stop immediately and find a pace that suits you.)

(2) Make yourself comfortable and imagine yourself to be in a place that gives you particular pleasure. Take time to enjoy the sounds, colours, scents, touch and temperature around you. Allow yourself to relax into it and stay there for as long as you can. When you return to your present surroundings remember that you can take yourself back again. Escaping physically or mentally, as a temporary break, can be helpful

in coping with stressful situations – unless it becomes a
habit of running away from difficulties.

(3) Find a comfortable floor and lie on your back, perhaps with
   a slim book under your head. Close your eyes and,
   beginning at the top of your head, work down your body
   progressively and slowly, relaxing the muscles in each area.

- Begin with your scalp, then work through your forehead,
  eyes, ears, jaws, cheeks, mouth, chin and neck.

- Move to one shoulder and down over the upper arm,
  elbow, lower arm, wrist, hand, fingers and let any tension
  drift out of the ends of your fingers.

- Work back up that arm slowly and move across to the
  other shoulder and do the same with that arm, ending back
  at your neck.

- Now work down your chest, making sure that you are
  breathing easily.

- Go down over your stomach to your pelvis and gently back
  up your front to your neck again.

- Now work down your back, thinking of the tension draining
  into the floor, over your shoulder blades, down each side
  of your spine, lower back and pelvis again.

- Begin with one hip and work down your thigh, knee, shin
  and calf, ankle, foot, toes and let any tension drift out of
  the ends of your toes.

- Now come back up that leg to your pelvis and do the same
  down the other leg.

- Move slowly back up that leg to your pelvis, feeling both
  your legs joining onto it, up to your waist, rib cage and
  back to your shoulders, feeling both your arms joining onto
  it, up your neck to your head and let any remaining tension
  drift out of the top of your scalp.

- Allow yourself to rest like this for as long as you can.

The whole exercise should be done slowly and should take at
least 20 minutes. Each person carries tension in different

places in the body so this is one way of finding out your own tension spots and learning how to relax completely.

There are different versions of this exercise:

- You can begin with your toes and end with your toes.

- You can begin with your head and end with your toes.

- You can begin with your toes and end with your head.

- You can tense each muscle area as you reach it before letting go.

- You can lie either with your legs stretched out or with your knees slightly bent.

- You can sit in a chair to do the exercise.

You might like to record these exercises for yourself on tape or buy one of the many relaxation tapes that are available.

References

Apple Computers/Henley Centre (1990) *Tomorrow's Business Priorities*. Report sponsored by Apple Computers UK and conducted by the Henley Centre.

Arthur Andersen (1991) *The Absenteeism Research Survey*, London.

Bird, D. (1992) 'Industrial stoppages in 1991', *Employment Gazette*, HMSO, May.

Boyes, P. (1987) 'A workplace problem', *The Director* (The Director Publications, London), July.

CBI/Department of Health (1992) *Prevention of Mental Ill Health at Work. A CBI and Department of Health Conference Report*. HMSO, London.

Coleman, V. (1992) 'Stress management', *Training and Development*, July.

Cooper, C.L. and Bramwell, R.S. (1992) 'A comparative analysis of occupational stress in managerial and shopfloor workers in the brewing industries', *Work and Stress*, Vol. 6, pp 127–38.

Cooper, C.L. and Sutherland, V.J. (1992) 'The stress of the executive life style: trends in the 1990s', *Employee Relations*, Vol. 13, No. 4.

Cooper, C.L., Sadri, G., Allison, T. and Reynolds, P. (1990) 'Stress counselling in the Post Office', *Counselling Psychology Quarterly*, Vol. 3, No. 1.

Fletcher, B. (1988) 'The epidemiology of occupational stress', in C.L. Cooper and R. Payne (eds) *Causes, Coping and Consequences of Stress at Work*, John Wiley and Sons.

Golembiewski, R.T. *et al.* (1986) *Stress in Organizations – Towards a Phase Model of Burnout*, Praeger, New York.

Hammond, V. and Holton, V. (1991) *A Balanced Workforce? Achieving cultural change for women: a comparative study*, Ashridge Management Research Group, Hertfordshire.

Handy, C. (1989) *The Age of Unreason*, Business Books.

Health and Safety Commission (1992) *Management of Health and Safety at Work – Approved Code of Practice*, HMSO, London.

Henley Centre (1988) *Planning for Social Change 1988*.

Henley Centre (1990) *Planning for Social Change Survey 1990*.

Henley Centre (1990) *Planning for Social Change 1990–1991*.

Herriot, P., Gibbons, P. and Pemberton, C. (1992) *An Empirical Model of Managerial Careers in Organisations*, Sundridge Park Management Centre, Kent.

Holmes, T.H. and Rahe, R.H. (1967) 'The Social Readjustment Rating Scale', *Journal of Psychosomatic Research*, Vol. 2, No.2.

Low Pay Unit (1992) 'Time off: a prize worth winning', *The New Review*, No. 14.

Megranahan, M. (1990) 'Employee Assistance Programmes: frameworks and guiding principles', *Employee Counselling Today*, Vol. 2, No. 3.

Mind National Association for Mental Health (1992) *The Mind Survey: Stress at Work*.

Munton, A.G. (1991) 'Managerial job relocation and stress: a 2-year investigation', MRC/ESRC, Social and Applied Psychology Unit, University of Sheffield.

Rosenman, R.H. and Friedman, M. (1975) 'Coronary heart disease in the Western Collaborative Group study', *Journal of the American Medical Association*, 233, pp. 872–7 (adapted).

Sports Council and Health Education Authority (1992) *Allied Dunbar National Fitness Survey*.

TUC (1988) *Hazards at Work*, TUC Publications.

Tuckman, B. (1965) 'Development sequences in small groups', *Psychological Bulletin*, Vol. 63, pp. 384–99.

Webb, S. (ed.) (1989) *Blueprint for Success: A Report on Involving Employees in Britain*, The Industrial Society, London.